18 Minutes

A Daughter's Primer on Life & Death

by

Susan MacNeil

WWW.OAKLEAPRESS.COM

18 Minutes: A Daughter's Primer on Life & Death © 2022 by Susan MacNeil. All rights reserved. No part of this book may be used or reproduced in any manner whatsoever without written permission except in the case of brief quotations embodied in critical articles and reviews. For information visit:

www.OakleaPress.com

On the cover: The author and her mother, November 2021

*"We are not human beings having a spiritual experience.
We are spiritual beings having a human experience."*
-Pierre Teilhard de Chardin

Dedicated to my mother, Jean Brady,

who for 90 years always led with her heart,

was the definition of kindness, compassion and love,

and still told me what to do as she lay dying during the last 18 minutes of her life.

Table of Contents

PROLOGUE: From Birth to Death 6

I. Saying Goodbye 8

II. When Mom Dies School 35

III. The Signs 47

IV. Concussion Psychosis 62

V. Taking Care of Business 72

VI. On Becoming a Motherless Child 78

VII. The Birthday Book 85

VIII. Visiting Hours 91

IX. Good Morning and Good Night 96

X. Funeral, Not Funeral 104

XI. Amplified Phones 119

Epilogue 135

Obituary 144

Photo Album 147

About the Author 152

PROLOGUE: From Birth to Death

Some say the creation of human life is a miracle. But what happens immediately after birth is the real phenomenon, where all the hard work will now be done independently by an unscathed being who has absolutely no idea what is to come.

Think about it. First, we are expelled from the womb, that voluptuous embrace of warmth and blood and nourishment on demand, where mother's body has been doing all the work for nine months. Then the umbilical cord lifeline is severed, and the very first moment of liberation takes place.

Water that fills the lungs is squeezed out by the pressure of sliding through the birth canal and is soon replaced by air. That first intake of breath forces the lungs to expand, resulting in a shrill cry of happiness, the welcome wagon of life. The shriek continues until breathing becomes normal. As infants, we are oblivious to the reality that this is the first of many crying jags to come.

Oxygen levels increase. Heartbeat strengthens. Eyes are wiped clear for an initial fuzzy view of this new place called home, which no doubt raises the question as to why departure from the sloshy, lovely, warm universe was necessary in the first place.

Skin color warms and changes from bluish purple to pink, weight and height are documented, fingers and toes are counted. A warm blanket enfolds us as we are brought to our creator. Five tiny fingers reach for the new umbilical cord known as our mother.

Then, the life-long journey begins.

In contrast, the last minutes of our lives are not predetermined. None of us know when or how the moment will come when our hearts will stop beating and our lungs will cease striving to take in air. If you are not at home, in your own bed, surrounded by the people you love when that time comes, you will likely be alone in a hospital or facility. There may be no time to be embraced by those who love you, no time to predict the moment when life, as you know it, ends.

Loved ones left behind will weep as you leave this earth, this physical plane of reality. They will feel as though their hearts are breaking, experience paralysis, barely able to move through and past their grief while managing your immediate, end of life needs. Their view of the world will change as salty tears create a hazy view, and they will wonder if the future can ever heal a fractured universe.

When they sit bedside to view your body after death, they will see no warmth. No movement. No fighting for air. No rosy apple cheeks. Only cold stillness. Afterward, they will wrap themselves in a blanket that once belonged to you. It will bring little comfort, but it will be something, nonetheless, especially if it's soft and pink.

Unable to reattach to a lifeline, the only thing that will remain the same as it was at birth are those ten fingers and ten toes. Grasping one of those beloved fingers for the last time, they will know an inexplicable memory, the first moment to say hello and the last to say goodbye.

Letting go for real.

Breathe in. Breathe out.

Gone.

1. Saying Goodbye

Oneness

The moment I die

I will try to come back to you

as quickly as possible.

I promise it will not take long.

Isn't it true

I am already with you

as I die each moment?

I come back to you

in every moment.

Just look,

feel my presence.

If you want to cry,

please cry,

And Know

that I will cry with you.

The tears you shed

will heal us both.

Your tears and mine.

The earth I tread this morning

transcends history.

Spring and Winter are both present in the moment.

The young leaf and the old leaf are really one.

My feet touch deathlessness,

And my feet are yours.

Walk with me now.

Let us enter the dimension of oneness

and see the cherry tree blossom in Winter.

Why should we talk about death?

I don't need to die

to be back with you.

Thich Nhat Hanh - Vulture Peak, India 2008

All I wanted was an amplified phone by Mom's bedside so she could hold an actual conversation. It escaped me why that was so hard to accomplish in a huge, capable facility like Hartford Hospital.

Her hearing had become increasingly diminished and was often the cause of laughter as she replied to a non-existent conversation, but it wasn't so funny when she was lying in a hospital bed.

"Mom, do you need to go to the market?" would translate to a response of, "The markers are in the pen drawer." This sort of non sequitur happened all the time. I threatened to get her one of those Victorian ear horns, the image of which made her laugh, but eventually she resorted only to leaning forward and pointing to her ear. Twenty-something wait staff would inevitably look at me after she signed this message, and I would reassure them it was okay to speak louder. It made me very uncomfortable to feel like I was yelling at my 90-year-old mother, and so I can imagine how they felt. I'd regularly state the obvious; that we needed to figure out how to find the money to get her a hearing aid. She would shrug her shoulders and apologize for the difficulty, which began five years earlier but was reaching a crescendo that had me researching the cost of various hearing aids. I did resort to purchasing an inexpensive earpiece but it was so tiny she wouldn't use it.

"What if it gets stuck in my ear canal while it's making that shrieking noise, and I can't fish it out?" Her fear was real and that meant she put it aside, hoping a day would come when she felt more courageous.

The incident that brought her via ambulance to the hospital terrified Mom. She was in her favorite small supermarket, happy to be out for an afternoon food run, when suddenly a sharp pain pierced her throat. She hated to bother anyone, and so she continued to push her cart up and down a few more aisles before she succumbed to the excruciating pain and growing inability to breathe. Mom went to the customer service desk and gasped. "Get me an ambulance."

Because angels seemed to follow her wherever she went, it made sense that a nurse overheard her and stayed with her until the ambulance arrived. The heart surgeon who saw her in the ER trauma unit said she likely had 24-48 hours to live and we should arrive sooner than later to say goodbye. Once he understood that I was her power of attorney and executor, we spoke bluntly about no extraordinary measures. He reiterated emphatically that she told him she was at peace.

Eventually I was able to speak with her, albeit briefly. The beep and whir of machines was in the background. Her breathing was labored and it was hard for her to hear me, especially given her degree of deafness. I sobbed and she provided the highlights. No extraordinary measures. Take care of everything we discussed, knowing this day would come. Make sure everyone is okay. Just go into neutral. You'll be okay. I love you all.

But 12 hours later the diagnosis had changed to the best of bad news. It wasn't her aortic aneurysm ready to explode; it was an aortic hematoma. A bruise on her beautiful heart. There was a possibility of managing this result with medication that lowered her blood pressure significantly, and so she was brought to the ICU, or the high roller suite as I referred to it. There, she had round the clock care, responsive nursing staff and lots of attention. When she needed an amplified phone, one appeared, and this brought extreme relief. Although the hospital had a Covid policy of one visitor per day for only 20 minutes, I was allowed to sit with her for an hour or more. I was glad she was still with us, and we clung to that phrase, "hopeful optimism."

Her doctor would call me daily with updates. None were great, but they held promise of improvement. Mom had already made an impression with everyone on staff including the doctor.

"We just love your mother. She is the sweetest, most kind person. So grateful for how we are able to help her. We really, really enjoy being with her." A terrified daughter longed to hear this over the phone.

Mom endeared herself to everyone, including the male aides. "Susan, you should see these strong young guys who help me. I never saw such a thing. They have tattoos all over their arms in the prettiest colors and designs. One even had Mom and Papa on his arm. Isn't that nice?" She told one of them how much she liked looking at his ink and he said she made his day.

I shared this story with her doctor who laughed like crazy. "Your mother's one of a kind."

That is who she was.

Four days later she stabilized enough to move to the cardiac floor below, which held many more patients than the ICU. While there she received tremendous attention, a necessity of being extremely ill and fragile. The double-edged sword occurred when she was moved out of ICU and to the cardiac floor, presumably to eventually go home.

Emotionally this was difficult for her, having to share a room with a very ill woman whose monitoring equipment beeped incessantly as all the while, the poor woman groaned. There was delayed access to nursing staff when she needed something. She felt like she was in a 'dungeon' because her space was smaller and she couldn't see out a window.

"I'm grateful for everyone here, and the nurses are so nice. But this bed is really uncomfortable. I'm cold all the time. I need that special pillow you bought for me. And the food needs to be hotter and taste better. I did have macaroni and cheese and meatloaf one night. It actually was good. So I will order it again. And I don't want them to be mad at me when I ask them for help, but it can take a long time to see someone after I ring the buzzer. So I just keep ringing it. In case they forgot. Not in a bad way. Just to remind them that I'm here. And you'd think they would take the covers off the pudding cups for you. That's hard to do when you're sick."

I'd brought her a velour jacket that she put on backwards so her arms could stay covered and her soft pink blanket, light as a feather, a gift from two Christmases ago. But she couldn't seem to warm up.

"My temperature also keeps going up to around 100, and I just know I have a bladder infection. I told them the name of the medication I take but the test keeps coming back negative. I know my own body. I'm old, but I know, so they ought to listen to me."

I made it my job to ask everyone who entered the room about the phone she needed. They promised to follow through. I figured it would be relatively simple to bring the one she had in the ICU down to her room. She wanted to call her loved ones, but it was a useless proposition to hold a one-way conversation and this was distressing to her, not to mention how disturbing it was for us to scream into the receiver. I promised to keep asking until we achieved success.

Before I left I tucked her under the blankets, pulled up the soft fluff of pink beneath her chin. She had received a number of compliments about her pretty hair and was happy her perm was holding up, despite being in bed.

"Do you think I'll get to go home on Wednesday?" she asked.

"The doctor wants to see more stability so likely not till Friday," I replied. "Should I cancel our mystery ride trip?"

She loved our mystery rides where I brought her to an unexpected location for a day or weekend. I'd planned one for Christmas, but the forecast of inclement weather caused me to cancel twice. The third reschedule was for the coming weekend; I wanted to give her the option of looking forward to the possibility.

"Well, tell me what it is so I know if I can really go." She grinned in excitement.

"Are you sure? It will ruin the surprise, Mom." She still became excited about gifts as though she was a child. It was part of her charm, this ability to savor every fun moment.

So I spilled the beans. "I'm going to pick you up on Saturday afternoon. We'll get to the Chesterfield Inn in New Hampshire around 4:30, just off 91 outside of Brattleboro. It's a short trip. You have a beautiful room reserved on the first floor with huge windows, lovely views and a fireplace. We'll get you settled, and then go down to dinner for 5:30. Justin is going to join us. Then I'll leave to go home, and return Sunday morning for breakfast, after which we'll head along to the Deerfield Inn, where we went for Thanksgiving. We have an 11:30 lunch reservation, and after that, we'll take a carriage ride down Main Street and into the woods."

She was smiling, her blue eyes sparkling and a look of wonder on her face as she clapped her hands together.

"How does that sound to you?" I asked.

"I hope they let me out of here so I can go," she replied. Who cares that a few days prior, a death sentence had hovered over her? She was game. She was always game for the next adventure.

"If they don't, I'll just keep rescheduling until we can make it happen. No problem, Mom."

It had been well over an hour and was time for me to go. I leaned down to stroke her cheek and kiss her forehead and eyes. "I love you, Mom."

"I love you, honey. Thank you for coming to see me." And she grabbed my hand which required another kiss on the velvet skin of hands that had done so much for us all.

"I think Don might come tomorrow, so he has a turn to see you. And I'll keep trying to get you an amplified phone by tonight or tomorrow morning." One more kiss, blown through the air, which she caught. "Love you. Sweet Dreams."

"Sweet Dreams, honey. Bye."

Our nightly emails to each other always ended with, "Sweet Dreams! Looooove." The extended o's in the word love was the result of a keyboard mistake she once made, and we simply continued this to express the sentiment, i.e., the more o's, the more love.

I was relieved that she had left ICU, but I was concerned the same strong oversight wasn't available. Still, I told myself that this was a sign of progress, and that I needed to worry less. I dutifully called the nurses station at 11 pm to follow up on my phone request and was told it still hadn't happened. Once more I asked specifically if the ICU could send down the phone to her floor. I reiterated how important it was, for all the obvious reasons, for Mom to be able to hear.

That night I willed the phone to appear and slept pretty well for six hours, until, that is, I awoke with a start at 7 am, Tuesday morning. It was odd how I jumped from a dream state to full alert. Immediately, I called to check on the phone and was told, again, that a phone was nowhere to be found. Nowhere in all four gigantic buildings of the hospital complex.

Now I was on it. Having been the Executive Director of an AIDS service organization for 15 years, I was unfortunately familiar with contacting hospital patient advocacy offices. So I got online, found the email address and composed the following email at 7:14 am on Tuesday, January 25.

Good Morning,

I am following up on the voicemail I left at 7 am regarding my mother, Jean Brady, who was moved from ICU yesterday to C10. She has been receiving excellent care, and I am grateful. But a seemingly simple request I've made five times since yesterday morning seems to be an impossibility.

Mom is very hard of hearing. She requires an amplified phone which she was provided in the ICU. Despite many requests, there is apparently not one of these phones to be found in the building. Last night around 11 pm I called to check and a phone still had not been found. I suggested that a phone be brought down from the ICU. But this morning I learned that this was not possible.

My mother's blood pressure after her heart incident is supposed to stay low. Our inability to communicate with her is only going to ensure that it remains too high. Under the ADA as well as from a compassionate perspective, a 90-yr-old woman needs to be able to speak with her family. I would appreciate your immediate attention to delivering an amplified phone to her room. And if this cannot be accomplished this morning, I will purchase one and bring it in. Otherwise, I fear a lack of communication will hamper her ability to leave the hospital.

Please contact me by 10 am so that I know how to proceed. Thank you for your prompt attention to this situation. -Susan MacNeil

I figured I wouldn't hear from anyone until midday and began to move into the kitchen to make coffee. Mom preferred an electric percolator, and I'd brought my own Bustelo espresso grind. I'd just put the inner parts in place when my cell rang.

It was 7:20 am. The number indicated Hartford Hospital. Instantly my heart lurched.

"Hello?"

"Susan? Can you hear me?"

"Mom, I'm sorry that they haven't brought the phone yet."

"Susan?"

Yelling now. "Yes, Mom. What's wrong?"

And then the sentence I will never, ever forget.

"I'm so sorry to have to tell you this, honey, but I think I'm dying."

My left arm froze in position with the phone to my ear.

"What? What's wrong?"

"Honey?"

"Oh, God, Mom, what's happening?"

"I can't hear you."

Screaming now, as loudly as I could while crying.

"Mom! I love you!"

"Dammit, I can't hear you. It's that pain. The one that I had before. It's starting again. The nurse came in to take my vitals and ran out of the room. No one is here now."

"I said I love you!"

"I love you too, honey. I'm so sorry."

"Mom! Mom!"

"Oh, God. It's bad. No one is here."

I couldn't feel my arm. I was aware that I was walking around the circular kitchen table in a loop, stopping in one spot to scream, then continue walking. At least I think I was walking. My view kept changing, but I couldn't feel my legs.

"Mom! I'm sorry! I hate that you are in pain! I love you!"

"So you know what to do. Pay the rent for February. I already paid the other bills for the month. Oh, God." Her breathing was now becoming more erratic.

"I will."

"And don't forget about the birthday book. That's your job now. Make sure that Auri gets that really cute Valentine's Day card I told you about."

"Yes. I will."

"Wait, here's someone. Hello? I need help. I am in pain. I'm in trouble."

An echoed voice replied. "Yes, I know. The nurse knows. She is trying to reach the doctor."

"Can't you do anything?" Mom pleaded.

"No, I am just an aide. The nurse needs instruction from the doctor."

"Oh, God, Susan. It's getting worse. I love you. Tell everyone I love them."

My brain turned on, and I grabbed the house phone with my right hand. Got through to the nurse's station.

"C-10, nurse's station."

"My mother is in room 63, and she's dying! And no one is there to help her! You need to go in there NOW! Please! Do something! She can't hear me because you didn't get the (expletive deleted) amplified phone and now she's dying!" I was on the verge of hysteria. And then, into my cell phone.

"I talked to the nurse. They are coming. I love you, Mom!"

"If this is how I have to live, not knowing when the excruciating pain will return, then I don't want to live."

"I love you!"

But her attempt at conversation was now over. I could hear her labored breathing punctuated by one word.

"Oh. Oh. Oh."

One last time I screamed at my mother. "Mom, I love you! I'm sorry! I love you!"

"I love you too, honey."

And then, click. The line went dead 18 minutes after she called.

I had no idea if she was alive or gone.

It was time to contact patient advocacy again. If I learned one thing from my years at AIDS Services, it was document, document, document.

7:40 am

I have just spent the most distressing 18 minutes of my life on the phone with my mother, who called to say that she was in the same excruciating pain that brought her to the hospital.

She was waiting for a nurse to arrive and called to say goodbye.

I could hear her.

She could not hear me unless I screamed ... Yes, I Will, I Love You.

Mom said that a nurse came in when she first reported the pain, took her vitals and ran out of the room.

Again, that was 18 minutes ago and no one but an aide returned.

Mom kept calling out for help.

No one came.

An aide entered the room and she repeated her need.

"I am in pain."

The aide said there was nothing to be done but wait for the nurse and the doctor's orders.

Mom's pain continued to escalate.

NO ONE CAME.

Finally I called the hospital on Mom's home phone at the same time and got through to the nurse's desk.

I told them of the situation and then nurses were sent to her room.

I then returned to my cell phone, but she was unable to speak.

My line was disconnected.

I am now waiting to hear from someone as to what happened.

Did she just die and was unable to actually have a final, loving conversation with me?

Are all your phone calls recorded?

If so, you should listen to the travesty of what just occurred.

UPDATE: Dr. Ahmed called to say that Mom was gone.

I told him what had happened, and he mentioned that shift change slowed things down.

Shannon, a nurse, called to have a kind conversation, reassuring me that Mom had a restful night.

She explained she had been on the phone with the doctor to find out next steps.

It was she who hung up the bedside phone.

I will be in by 10 am to see Mom before she goes to the morgue.

Contact a wealthy donor and buy enough amplified phones so that a final conversation can occur in a respectful, loving manner.

I'm glad to know that Mom's last night on earth was restful.

But the last 18 minutes of her life were spent in escalating pain unable to actually hear my voice. –Susan

Just like that, one hour after I awoke with a start, the doctor called to tell me that Mom had died. My left arm had been so frozen from holding the phone that a cramp prevented me from straightening it. Dr. Ahmed heard my plea about the horror of my last 18 minutes with Mom and agreed it was an issue that needed to be addressed. He tried to explain what happened medically, but I couldn't take it in. I asked to speak with him when I got to the hospital so I could sit with Mom one last time, and he said he would be available. He expressed his condolences.

And that was it.

I was in shock, but I couldn't remain in a state of oblivion because I now had to be the daughter in charge, the oldest sister. The executor of Mom's estate. Immediately, I had to let my brothers know and my son know, regardless of how surreal the moment seemed. Others could wait.

I made the decision, consciously, to put aside the details of our final conversation and to focus instead on how lucid she was, still providing direction and making sure we all knew she loved us right up to the end. Those 18 minutes were my burden to assimilate in the moment, because I recalled a very specific instruction from When Mom Dies School.

"Make sure everyone is okay."

When I had gotten the original call from the ER five days prior, and we thought we were saying goodbye, I could barely speak. Her last words to me then were equally wise.

"Just go into neutral. You'll be okay. I love you all."

So my next steps were clear.

Go into neutral. And make sure everyone can cope.

Got it.

I wore my hair down because my mother loved it that way. One bonus of the pandemic lockdown is that many of us got to grow out our hair. So I decided to take advantage of staying in the house where no one could see me during those awful months of a short cut becoming long, determined to one day be an old lady with gray locks worn on the top of my head or in a braid.

Mom adored my long hair growing up. My childhood ponytail was one big fat curl that swung from side to side when I walked. Pin curl bangs were painstakingly put in place, her fingers slippery with gel before ensuring the spirals would stay in shape under the X-shaped bobby pins.

But today there was no special care. It's not clear to me how I took a shower, put myself together, drove into Hartford and was able to communicate with the valet guy, the woman at the admissions desk, the security guard who saw my tears and reached out to me.

"Mother?" he asked.

I nodded.

"Me, too. We're gettin' 'bout to bury her. My condolences, dear."

In the elevator I lost the ability to comprehend the number pad. As others called out their floor I could not speak.

A nurse who clearly was familiar with the state of shock I was in asked, "What floor, honey?"

"The cardiac one," I replied through my tears as she pushed the button.

"Hang on. You'll be okay."

My mother's room was actually located in the corner of the floor so that when I reached her hallway I could simply turn right. And there she was.

I hadn't been to an open casket funeral in a long time, but there is no comparison between seeing a body dressed in best clothes, a little make-up, surrounded by flowers … and your mother just after she has died. Immediately I noticed that her skin was already jaundiced, just 2 hours after she was gone. Her mouth was wide open and that was disturbing. The chaplain was waiting for me, Father Richard, and it was clear he had lots of experience in his job. He asked me all the right questions.

What was her faith? Did she believe in God? Had we discussed her wishes? There were more, but I think his intention was to keep me talking so that I didn't completely drift away. All I knew was that he was Catholic, this would make Mom happy, and he could administer the last rites per her request. As he sprinkled holy water over her, I recalled the rituals of every Sunday church service I attended as a child. The Latin mass. The kneeling. The swinging gold container full of smoky incense as the priest approached the altar. The mystery of communion. And how important it was to look your Sunday best.

Mom would hate that she hadn't dressed for church at her final service.

Shortly after I arrived, two nurses came into the room and stood at her bedside. You could tell they were experienced in managing this moment. One was clearly the head nurse, her sweater covered in all kinds of pins meant to indicate her status. The other was the charge nurse. They expressed their condolences with genuine care, and I waited until they had finished before unleashing my sorrow which was not couched in anger but pain, punctuated by breathless sobs.

"Just tell me one thing. Why couldn't you have brought her an amplified phone? Since yesterday morning, I've asked six people. I could hear her, but she couldn't hear me unless I screamed into the phone. I stood in my mother's kitchen for 18 minutes and yelled I love you at the top of my lungs over and over again. She couldn't hear the tone of my voice. We couldn't have a final conversation. Do you understand how important this is?"

They nodded and agreed that it was a terrible situation. The head nurse said, "You're right. I've bumped up the issue to admin." As if this was supposed to make me feel better. The nebulous admin. Like the Wizard of Oz behind the curtain.

I couldn't stop. "Why didn't a nurse come to be with her those last 18 minute as her pain increased? What were you doing while she was dying?"

The charge nurse now replied. "We were trying to reach the doctor. We got here when you called us. I was the person who hung up her phone."

I was done being an adult and began to moan. "But she couldn't hear me. She couldn't hear my voice. In this whole huge hospital, you couldn't find a phone for her? Just one phone? I'll never be able to get over this."

The nurses both expressed sympathy once more and repeated that some removed person who lived in the world of admin was going to look into it. Yeah, right.

I asked the head nurse if she could do something about Mom's mouth being agape. I was struck by what a good job Mom had done taking care of her teeth. She was at the dentist regularly and had an arrangement with him to pay $60/month to cover any work she might need. Every doctor, dentist, chiropractor, nail technician, beautician and staff person answering the phone in any office appreciated and remembered my mother. They went out of their way to provide her comfort as well as to become her friend. Of course, it might have been because they coveted her blueberry muffins, handwritten notes in thank you cards or being called 'honey' by a sweet woman from a generation that didn't abide by political correctness. A personal connection made with my mother was not easily forgotten.

The nurse returned with a rolled up towel and tried to close Mom's mouth, but apparently this becomes very difficult immediately after death. I watched frozen as she carefully edged the towel upward to do what she could. I couldn't decide if I felt revulsion or gratitude. A small improvement was accomplished and that had to be good enough.

They left the room so I could be alone, and I stayed for over an hour. I held her hand. I stroked her hand. I kissed her hand. I cried. I took pictures of our hands together and of her face. When

I focused the camera on her face I almost turned away, yet I required this image to remind myself that she was gone. It wasn't gruesome. It was saying goodbye. And I needed that.

But what struck me in the moment, and what remains with me now is the absolute truth that our bodies are only a shell for our spirit. It was her beautiful heart that turned this still husk into a living, breathing, loving human being. The beauty industry tries to get us to believe that our bodies are what matters most, permeating the culture with a false assumption of worth, according to our reflection in the mirror.

But this simply is not true.

The chaplain came and went, checking to make sure I was okay. Someone brought me water. I was frozen in my chair at her bedside. I remember thinking, so this is what it's really like when Mom dies. Not the intellectual exercise about funeral homes and burial plots and insurance policies and money concerns and a million pieces of paper in large clasp envelopes. Not the conversational instructions that she shared with me. But this.

And those last 18 minutes.

Dr. Ahmed was young, knowledgeable and compassionate. He explained the heart scenario that likely occurred to cause Mom's death. Pericardial effusion. Fluid from the aortic hematoma had built up around her heart and prevented it from working. A black and blue surrounding the organ that kept her alive. He asked if I wanted her to go through an autopsy and I told him it wasn't necessary; that she preferred not to have one unless it was somehow important. He agreed and felt there was no cause for her death other than the one he identified.

I thanked him for the top-notch medical care that had extended her life for seven days. And then I circled back to what was most important.

Those 18 minutes.

He agreed that it was a terrible thing for Mom and I to go through but he wanted me to know that at the moment of death she died peacefully, without trauma. I'm not sure how he quantified 18 minutes of increasing pain and the knowledge that this was it, her last moments, unable to hear my voice with the word, peace. He also said that during shift change things slow down and likely that was why no one was immediately in the room with her.

Got it. Don't die in the hospital when it's time for a shift change.

He also recommended that I try not to focus on our final heart-wrenching interaction because he was sure that she could hear what I was saying and knew that I loved her. He asked me to congratulate her 90 years and her sharp mind and her loving spirit, all of which is true. He mentioned that she was impressively lucid. When she insisted that the ongoing temperature issue was due to a bladder infection and told him what antibiotic to order – levofloxacin – he ran one more test.

The first two had come back negative. The third one was positive. She was right.

I knew what he was trying to do. I appreciated it. I had no quarrel with the medical care she received. But if something as simple as having a proper phone in a patient's room so they can feel connected to their world is so daunting, then this is one critical piece that requires attention. All I could think of was … how many other elderly, hard of hearing patients and their loved ones will experience the same thing? And how much Mom would have hated that.

Eventually another patient was brought into the room to fill the bed, and I knew it was time for me to go. I kept trying to stand up from the chair but couldn't straighten my knees. My brain and heart were not in sync. It was only when they fully positioned this woman's bed, hooked up her machines and I heard the electronic pulse of her heartbeat that I was struck by the inalienable fact that my mother's heart had stopped beating and would not begin again.

With a final need for acceptance I stood, went around to her bedside as I did the day before and once again kissed her forehead, her cheek, her eyes. Then I reached for her hand with one last hold, one last kiss. I always thought this would be a maudlin exercise, but it was comforting to the five-year-old who didn't want her mommy to die.

Somehow, I turned to leave the room and was met by the chaplain. I asked him about her belongings which needed to be placed in neon green plastic bags, the ones provided for patients leaving the hospital. He ran to get the nurse team and they assured me they would take care of the task.

I asked if he would accompany me to the chapel to wait, and he agreed. I had no real desire to do so, but I knew that Mom would like that. So down he went, with me following behind. We opened the door and then I immediately realized why I had been compelled to go here.

It was the quote on the wall as we walked in. The same words that were on the bumper sticker on Mom's car. The words that informed her world view.

"We are not human beings having a spiritual experience. We are spiritual beings having a human experience."

I knew this was my first after-death message from Mom. Inside, the space was peaceful, and I was alone. A maroon orchid stood in the sunlight of the stained glass window. The chaplain sat at the back of the room. Almost immediately both nurses arrived with three bags and a parking validation ticket to give to the valet. Together we walked outside. A conversation with the valet ensured that he would place the bags in my car for me. The trio said goodbye, and it was over.

Mom was officially gone. But the new normal had officially begun. I took a picture of the view from the main entrance as I waited for my car to be brought around. The first view of the outside world living in the new normal.

Thirty minutes later, I was back in her kitchen, the very spot where I had stood that morning. Instead of hours, it felt like I'd been away for a month. I took a moment to gaze at my surroundings. This space, her space that she loved so much, now seemed empty, meaningless, yet somehow, it was still filled with her life force.

Since I had been staying in her place, sleeping in her bed while she was hospitalized, she'd asked how I liked it during one of our visits.

"It's pretty nice, isn't it? Comfortable. Safe. I've been so happy here."

Tears had stopped flowing for a moment as I remembered that conversation. Then the phone rang. Caller ID indicated it was Hartford Hospital. Suddenly I couldn't feel my face.

"Hello," was my dull reply.

"Hi, is this Susan MacNeil? This is Maria from patient advocacy. You emailed us this morning. I wanted to let you know that we are working on getting a phone for your mother."

I was all out of politeness, now. "Gee, thanks, but you're too late. Apparently you didn't read your email thoroughly." I paused for effect, aware that I was creating discomfort. I wanted her to feel as badly as I did. I didn't care that it wasn't the right thing to do.

"Mom is dead. She doesn't need a phone any longer."

Five long seconds of silence were followed by, "We got an email from this morning but I didn't see another one."

"Then I guess you didn't read carefully enough," I replied. "I'll forward it to you so you have the full conversation."

I heard her say, "I'm really sor..." as I hung up the phone and went to Mom's computer to forward the most important part of the conversation.

"Damn patient advocacy," I yelled aloud to no one. I looked at all the pieces of paper taped all over Mom's computer, a jumble of internet user names and passwords she had tried to keep track of but somehow never managed to find when she needed them most.

"Damn patient advocacy," I whispered as I disappeared into my tears.

II. When Mom Dies School

"We are not human beings having a spiritual experience.

We are spiritual beings having a human experience."

-Pierre Teilhard de Chardin

It was 2016 and my mother was 85. I organized a surprise birthday party for her by taking her on yet another mystery ride. It was hard to choose the location but I knew it had to be in Massachusetts so that her extended family could attend.

As a teenager I was fascinated with a story she told about visiting her aunt who lived in Rockport. The house was close to the ocean, and Mom slept in a four-poster bed. To my mind it sounded perfectly elegant, although she said it was just an old metal bed with squeaky springs centered against the inside wall. Facing her were two windows that were left open so she could sleep comfortably.

One night there was a huge thunderstorm, and as her 12-year-old frame lay tucked under the covers in fear, the impossible happened. She saw a bolt of lightning come into the room through one window, touch all four corners of each poster and leave out of the second window.

I was always fascinated with this story because it sounded impossible, but I knew it was true. After all, it happened to my mother! Surviving the near embrace of lightning made it seem like the hand of God himself had been her protectorate, and this made her unbelievably powerful in my eyes.

But the event traumatized her. Years later, when we were young and my father was working second-shift at Pratt & Whitney, she would herd us all into the living room to sit in fear of the thunder and lightning roaring outside. Clutching the 'important papers' in her hand, she would lead us in song. I never really knew what those papers were for, except that if we were to die, someone needed to find them. "Old MacDonald had a farm, e-i-e-i-o..."

One time our car, which should have been in the Pratt & Whitney East Hartford parking lot, was in the driveway. I don't know where my father was, but we were alone and ran from the kitchen through torrential rain to get inside... because it had rubber tires. The important papers got wet, but they survived and so did we.

I recall one rare occasion when a tornado was predicted, and the sky turned that odd shade of green-brown. Like lemmings, we followed Mom down the street to huddle in the root cellar of 'Old Mrs. Glenney' – no disrespect intended. That is what we called her, because to us she seemed to be at least 100 years old. I will never forget the dank humidity, the earthy smell, the low dirt ceiling, and jars of preserved pickles and vegetables lined on wooden slabs which posed as shelves. The items inside the glass containers were barely identifiable because of the thick cover of dust. I recall running my finger over the outside of one jar to see inside.

Beets. We didn't eat beets in our house.

Over the years Mom had talked about enjoying and missing Rockport, so that was the designated gathering point. And we carried it off – she never suspected a thing. It was a wonderful party filled with lasting memories. But on the way home, the reason for the occasion didn't escape our conversation. She was now 85 years old. Doing very well, considering, but adjusting to the reality of approaching the end of her life. Mom tried to bring up the tricky subject with me, but I wasn't having it.

Except that I wasn't stupid. Now it was real. Eighty-five meant she was going to die sooner or later - maybe sooner, but hopefully later - and there were things we needed to discuss.

A year passed and like clockwork just before her 86th birthday, the conversation returned. One minute we were on the phone planning her birthday mystery ride, and the next minute, she brought the sledgehammer down.

"Now Susan, I'm getting old. I don't think I'm going to die anytime soon. But I will die. So you and I have to go to 'When Mom Dies School.'"

Immediately, tears replaced my happy tone, but that didn't stop her. "Don't be sad. I'm still in pretty good health. But I need to show you the important papers (there was that phrase again) to spell out my wishes, and what you will need to do when I die."

I later learned that her beloved senior center had brought someone in to talk about what needs to be in place for the eventual end of life moment. And my mother, ever a good student, and someone who acted on necessary information, responded in her, and in our, best interest.

The following years found us discussing these details more and more. We muddled through various end of life templates provided as helpful starting points. She reiterated how she never wanted to be intubated, or have CPR, because she'd heard that it cracked your ribs. She didn't want extreme surgeries or life-prolonging measures unless there was real hope, and certainly not if she would linger for more than three months. Most of all, she feared being unable to communicate. She could not imagine a worse possible outcome. And because she hated anyone she loved to suffer in any way, she did not want us to be standing at her bedside in prolonged grief.

As the eldest daughter, I was to be the executor and power of attorney for Mom. This was not at all surprising to me, but the more we contemplated the eventuality, the more daunting it felt. In order to try to make it incrementally real, I decided to order additional copies of every good photo that resulted from our many outings over the next four years so that I'd have them for the eventuality of her death.

Mom didn't understand the technology that allowed my phone to also be a serious camera. We grew up with her always taking photos, a camera by her side. Inevitably her finger would get caught up in her hair, or miss the button, or accidently turn it off, and we would be stuck with frozen smiles on our face until she was happy with the image. But she loved being on the other side of the camera and would readily pose anywhere, at any time. I'd instruct her as though we were professionals.

'Tilt your chin down. Turn a little to the left with your shoulder. Not so many teeth."

The deal was that I would then show her the pictures and she would have final approval. She needed instant gratification, our standard operating procedure. "Oh, that one's good. But no, delete that one. Do it now. I don't want that on Facebook." We'd laugh at her vanity, I'd post it on Facebook to both her page and mine, and then throughout the remainder of the day I'd show her the growing comments from her admirers.

Once the copies arrived, I'd stash them in a bag in my photo album chest, the intention being to have her approved copies available for guests at her eventual funeral. Beautiful, smiling, memories of happy times as a remembrance of who she was. Not one of those staged, frozen images from a Sears photo session, but Mom in real life, having fun.

At first, I'd cry each time I added pictures to the bag, but after a couple of years it became easier. We went on many trips together and I told myself it was like a school assignment – gather up all the pretty photos of Mom that I could possibly find and save them to give away when we needed to remember who she was and how she lived.

I was so glad I had done this when the moment finally arrived. Just after Mom's death, I was sitting with my oldest childhood friend when I recalled my plan.

"Wait a minute! I told you about the photos I've been saving, right?" I jumped up and pulled out stacks of pictures from the bag in no particular order. There must have been close to 300 jumbled on the table. The matching game of all matching games for heartsick daughters.

It was a good two-hour distraction.

Five days prior, when the ER trauma doctors said she had 24 hours to live, I ran to the important papers of When Mom Dies School. Instantly, I realized that although I'd been collecting every document carefully through the years, I'd not actually organized them. Insurance policies were scattered amongst power of attorney papers. There were medical and financial instructions, confirmation that I was co-signatory on her checking account. Burial plot details. Specifics from her visit to the funeral home to choose a casket and determine her final plans. Notes about what I should do first, second, third.

In that moment I realized it had been a way for me to avoid the inevitable while seeming to be on top of things. It was the best gift she ever gave to me, this roadmap to the end of her life. I stayed up all night hoping that additional medical tests would bring us the best of bad news, while setting about the task that could no longer be ignored.

And we got lucky when she ended up in ICU, each day meant for improvements to bring her closer to discharge. I dutifully brought the now organized file folder with the pretty blue and purple floral design to the hospital so we could review them. Which we did, briefly.

"You've got it all there. And we've talked about everything a lot. So take some time and let me know if you have any questions." Then she grabbed my hand. The conversation was over.

Her implicit belief that this was just another day at school made me both nervous and hopeful. It seemed to me that if she didn't feel the pressing need to review each document, then it must mean she would come home soon. I tried to hold both thoughts in my head simultaneously. *Coming home* was easy to do at her bedside. *Dying* began the need for deep breathing to avoid hyperventilation.

Actually. Dying. Because all people are mortal. And die.

I pored over the contents of the file repeatedly so as not to have missed anything. To prepare for any eventuality, while she was still in ICU, I emailed the funeral home with questions about the contract Mom had created. It was my idea of a dry run. Twelve hours later I had an email in return which brought some peace of mind that the funeral director was aware of this document, remembered my mother, and was confident he would be prepared in the event of her death. It was comforting to know that this stop on the roadmap existed and was awaiting our arrival.

In hindsight I am filled with gratitude that the medical team at Hartford Hospital kept her alive for five days. They approached her care with the idea that she would stabilize and be able to go home, which was all she talked about.

I reminded her that I was unrelenting in my attempt to find her another amplified phone. "Just do what you can. It's not nice to make people scream into the phone. I'd like to be able to talk like normal."

On day three I realized the one thing we never did was a will. I jumped onto Law Depot to create the document. This is a very important resource to know about because you can find any template you need at your fingertips. The cost is reasonable – the will was $49.95. I completed it easily since Mom didn't own anything, have a stash of money somewhere, and told me if any money was left over from the insurance policies I was to share it fairly. On Monday, her fourth day of hospitalization and now out of ICU, I brought it in so we could review it together. I'd hoped to get her approval and if so, find a notary to sign it at her bedside.

But she wouldn't hear of it. Being moved out of ICU meant she was getting better. She would be home soon. Definitely by the weekend. And we could look at it then so she could focus without interruption.

At that moment I succumbed to her desire and intention; that she would be back in her sweet apartment and we would sit at her kitchen table with freshly baked blueberry muffins to talk it through.

If she had an estate with real property and abundant assets, this would have been the wrong decision. But weighing the perfunctory nature of a will against bolstering her desire to live, I erred on the latter.

I don't regret it. Even though she died the next morning. To the end she felt she was going to come home and that kept her moving forward. She was always my biggest cheerleader. Now I was going to be hers.

At 68 years of age, when your 90-year-old mother is really ill and possibly dying, it doesn't matter that you think you are plenty old enough and prepared to do all the necessary tasks associated with their demise. You can tell yourself that as long as you've had the big conversation, know her wishes, and understand how the important papers determine the responsibility of your role as executor, you're good to go.

But this is an intellectual assumption. Trying to move forward to do all the tasks in front of you, as quickly and seamlessly as possible, while you are also experiencing this depth of grief is akin to slogging through quicksand. One minute you think you're going to make it out of the quagmire. The next moment you are being sucked down into a black hole.

And you become a motherless child, sinking into the depth of despair and hopelessness heard in the traditional African American spiritual from the late 1800s. Not the Eric Clapton version. Nor the Richie Havens version. The original.

Now I have been told by some friends who don't have a close relationship with their mother that the death of a parent was simply an expectation and out of their control. It was sad, of course, but not traumatic. In my case, there were those 18 minutes at the end of Mom's life. And the decision I'd made not to immediately share them with my brothers and my son meant that I carried this all alone, at least for the time being.

I did so because Mom told me to "make sure everyone is okay." She was famous for holding onto bad news until it had improved. She was a big fan of, "Just think about four weeks from now when things will be better."

So, for my brothers, I had to consider that my youngest brother, Bruce, was not doing well. My oldest brother, Bill, was dealing with his wife undergoing a second round of radiation treatment in Florida for cancer, as well as her mother dying the same week as Mom. The result was that their three children lost both grandparents in the span of five days. And my next oldest brother, Don, was a gem who brought energy and thoughtfulness to the situation, but had been completely devoted to Mom and was deeply mourning.

My son, Justin, her first and dearly held grandchild, was lovingly pragmatic about Mom's passing and had fortunately recently spent quality time with her. The night of her ER admission, I'd called to check on the visitation policy and was told that it was one person per hour per patient for 20 minutes maximum in both ICU and on the general floors. He drove over 3 hours to the hospital the day after she was admitted only to discover that the visiting policy had changed to one person per patient per day.

Because of the pandemic.

He gave up his chance to visit her in favor of me since I was her executor and she was so ill. But as it turned out, Bruce had also driven hours to get there. He hadn't checked his text messages to see the ongoing conversation about visitation planning until he was almost at the hospital. I knew Mom would want him to see her given the circumstances, so I gave him my spot.

Meanwhile, Justin's reaction to doing the right thing, but not being able to see his grandmother was to have a very loud and, some might say, inappropriate conversation in the lobby on the phone with her. This is how she relayed what he said.

"Poor Justin was so upset that he couldn't come to see me. He called me and he was yelling, saying the g.d. word and the f. word.

Not at me, the g.d. word, but at the hospital and the visitation rules. I was worried he was going to get arrested. He told me he loved me and was sending a piece of chocolate cake to my room. I understand he was just frustrated. The pandemic, you know, makes it harder for everyone."

Afterward Justin told me that a nurse who was walking by overheard his plight – I'm sure he drew the attention of everyone in the lobby – and said she would be happy to take the cake to Mom in the ICU, which she did. But to tell him the horror of those last 18 minutes before he had some time to process her death? Absolutely not.

He had already made it clear he would not be attending the private family visiting hours with an open casket. He had no desire to see her dead. I remember being in the room with both of my deceased grandmothers, full open casket, simply unable to go up to the kneeler and look down upon their faces. It was bad enough to get a view from the back of the room. My Catholic aunts were appalled.

But my mother calmly said, "Leave her alone."

So if Justin didn't want to see my mother's body with her spirit missing, it was fine with me. And I decided to hold onto these terrible details of her last 18 minutes until her celebration of life in the spring, when I would give them the option of reading my recollection of that terrible day. And I would give myself the opportunity to have carried and managed the burden alone, without their additional grief and pain.

I was just following Mom's instructions to make sure everyone was okay. And that included me.

III. The Signs

Epitaph

"And when you need me,

Put your arms around anyone

And give them what you need to give me.

Love doesn't die, people do.

So when all that's left of me is love,

Give me away."

-Merritt Malloy

I am a big believer in paying attention to the signs that are all around us. So was Mom. Daily messages that appear to inform us from beyond. Instruct us how to move through the difficulties and sadness of our lives. And provide a plan to go forward. I wasn't sure there was a heaven, but I do believe that there is a God who loves us. As Mom always said, God isn't mean. So we should not judge others.

Love was her doctrine.

Every dragonfly that flitted around her as she lay outside to enjoy the breezes of a sunny afternoon was really the visit of a lost loved one. Her intuition and dreams delivered important information and comfort. She was not afraid about the end of her life. Her faith informed her that she would be reunited with loved ones and then be able to watch over all of us forever.

In the fall of 2021 she began to remark about regularly seeing cardinals, those blood-red birds attached to a rich folklore of meanings: harbingers of a spiritual emissary, visits from a departed soul, reminder that angels are near, love, life, happiness. They even visited her in dreams about her long-departed mother and father.

I never told her that these revelations made me nervous, portending access to the spirit realm. When she saw an ad on Facebook for a tabletop adornment resembling a birch tree, with branches and fairy lights and cardinals delicately balanced on each slim branch, it delighted her.

"Would you like this?" I asked, overcoming my trepidation. Of course she did, so I ordered the tree and package of feathery cardinals to be sent to her home. I told myself I was being silly. It was just a lovely holiday centerpiece. That's all.

Until I visited her a few weeks later for Christmas. I opened the door and the first thing I saw were the twinkling lights surrounding eight perched cardinals. Decorating for Christmas was one of her favorite things to do, placing antique Santa's and elves amidst all the cards she received.

A vibrant image was replicated on the table beneath the birch branches. Instantly I realized that these cards were all the same.

"The display is beautiful, Mom. Did you buy the cards to go along with it?"

No, she said. The cards were from six people who didn't know one another. The very same card, each featuring the image of a beautiful cardinal.

"Isn't that funny?" she asked.

"It's very odd," I replied, a chill going through me. My breath caught momentarily as the thought went through my head that she was soon going to die. But I refused to accept the message, because we had made a pact that she was going to live to at least 95. Five more years of mystery rides and flowers and gifts. That was our plan.

One month later when I entered her apartment as she lay in the ICU, the cardinal display taunted me.

"Not yet, please. Not yet," I declared aloud.

Five days after her death I made sure to take the cardinal display home with me, at once fearful of their power and bereft in their message. I placed the branch on the kitchen table and turned on the lights.

"Show me some signs, Mom. Help me get through this," was my daily prayer. I decided it was important to keep a list of all the signs that were provided in my hours of need.

Tuesday, 1/25 – The day she died. After I sat with her for an hour I was compelled to ask the chaplain to lead me to the chapel while I awaited delivery of her belongings. I didn't know why until we walked in the room. And there, on the wall, in huge lettering, was her favorite saying. Her bumper sticker. It was the first sign Mom gave to me and she had only been gone four hours.

"We are not human beings having a spiritual experience. We are spiritual beings having a human experience."

During the trip home I did have an awareness that I needed to stop texting while flying down the highway at 75 mph because I was swerving between lanes. But the actual driving? A blank, except that along the way four hawks swooped in front of my view. Hawks are sacred messengers and their wisdom was simple.

Slow down. Stop texting. Pay attention.

Wednesday, 1/26 – As I wept at my kitchen table feeling like I couldn't go on, I needed a sign. A bowl of ceramic stars sat on the table, each one inscribed with a word. I dumped the bowl, turned the stars upside down, closed my eyes and moved my fingers over the shapes until vibrations determined my choice.

The word on the star was, Accept. Exactly what I needed to do, and was so far from doing.

"Okay, Mom. If you insist. I'll try."

Thursday, 1/27 – I had grabbed folders and files Mom had earmarked for this day, not really knowing what I would find. Mom had specifically asked me not to simply toss the items inside but "respectfully" take the time to look at each piece of paper.

There were two signs today. One was a gratitude list, the other a handwritten note to the eventual new tenants for her apartment once she was gone. Pre-pandemic, as part of When Mom Dies School, we discussed a move from Connecticut to Vermont so she could be close to me. A lovely housing complex, which was once the hotel for train and mill workers, sat two blocks down from my place in our little village. Located on the first canal built in the United States, there were sweeping views of the mountains and water. The train came through twice a day with its whistle notifying arrival at the station. On her visits she found our little downtown engaging with its many storefronts, brick and Italianate architecture, Opera House and clock tower. The notion delighted her of walking from the old-fashioned hardware store, complete with squeaky wooden floors, to the coffee shop at the head of the square.

We had many conversations about what this would look like, how momentous it would be for her to leave Connecticut after living there since 1950. I shared information about our senior center, health center, and area hospitals. My encouragement included the promise of being able to enjoy an outing every weekend instead of every 6-8 weeks. In the end, the decision was entirely hers.

I expected her reply to take months, but after only three weeks she called me to say that she had made a decision.

"This makes sense. You are my power of attorney and executor. I should be close to you in case anything happens. It's my last big adventure." And that was it.

It was 2019. She began the process of packing and filled out the apartment housing application so it could be submitted two months before she would depart. She told her doctors about the plan and asked them to recommend their Vermont counterparts so she could have her lifeline in place upon arrival.

Mom was 88 years old and committed. Her enthusiasm about the future was contagious. We were both looking forward to the big day, and then ... the world changed in a heartbeat when we learned the words, Covid-19. By the time summer 2020 rolled around, the window of opportunity had closed.

"Honey, we need to talk about my move. I just don't think it's a good idea given this new, terrible disease. The advice is to stay in your homes and don't go out unless you have to. No-one knows when it will end. What do you think?"

And I had no choice but to agree. We joked about how she had a wall of boxes already lined up in her spare room, but since they were not labeled she had no idea what was inside each one. However, since she apparently wasn't missing those items, she figured she didn't need them anyway.

I thought a lot about this moment in time, our best laid plan, when I was headed to ICU.

Friday, 1/28 – One of the last instructions Mom gave me had to do with her Birthday Book. The spiral-bound monthly minder came with pockets for pending cards and a date grid so that the names of recipients could be written next to their special day.

Mom loved cards. It is fair to say she was a Hallmark fanatic. She came from a generation when sending a card was a very big deal. It meant you were sending love. The more expensive, the bigger the card, the lovelier the verse, the greater the love.

In the months before she died she also had discovered LovePop cards. These cards boasted top of the line, magical surprises. They opened up to feature an expanded 3-D image, anything from butterflies to roses. She loved the little tab on the right that, when pulled, provided the blank space upon which to write your message so it didn't ruin the artistry inside.

The birthday book included the names of friends, relatives and the birthdays of loved ones who had passed. She would draw a heart next to their name to indicate they were gone, but she still recognized their role in her life.

This compendium was a treasure trove of my family. She knew the names and addresses of every child belonging to her deceased sister and brother, and their children as well. She would often speak to me of them although I had no idea who they were.

"I found the best card for (fill in the blank.)" or "Today I spent the afternoon doing the birthday cards for (fill in the month.)" Once I asked her how much money she thought she spent on cards and stamps.

"I never think about it. I just do it," was her reply.

In her final moments as I stayed on the phone with her, I received very specific instructions about the Birthday Book, which also included Valentine's Day cards. She had already begun to purchase some for the February love event, instructing me which card was to go to which great-grandchild. And reminded me that this family responsibility was now mine.

That afternoon when I needed distraction from end of life paperwork, I turned to the Birthday Book. I still hadn't received a sign from Mom and was about to let it go. But there, in the pocket, I found a stack of cards, specific valentines she mentioned. And one more.

Mine.

It was not signed but the message was clear. She was always thinking ahead. Nestled in a floral heart on the front of the card, these words embraced me.

"Daughter, I want to give you a few simple words to carry in your heart every day."

And inside, "I love you, believe in you, and admire you. You've made my life meaningful in a way that nothing else could, and I just can't imagine a world without you. Happy Valentine's Day." Classic Hallmark.

The message could not have been a more beautiful way to help me go forward. Unsigned, she hadn't yet penned a note because it was still mid-January. But she had spotted the perfect card and brought it home to make sure it awaited her attention. I wondered if she directed me to the birthday book for this reason.

As I sat wailing at the kitchen table, feeling rather desperate, I reached for the stars again. I hoped for another word like Accept, something profound that would propel me from this place of grief.

But that was not in her playbook. I followed the ritual, chose the star, and turned it over.

It commanded me to Laugh. Which I did. As loudly as I had been wailing.

Saturday, 1/30 – Moving forward to address Mom's death had become my job. I'd give myself time in the morning to get up whenever, drink espresso and randomly move things from one place to the other. When I felt I was ready, I assumed the position at the table and opened yet another 9x12 clasp envelope or folder.

The night Mom was admitted to the ICU on January 18, I didn't sleep. I poured over the When Mom Dies School paperwork and eventually sat down to write a draft obituary. I considered it a practice run that I'd squirrel away for another day in five years when it became necessary.

But try as I might, I couldn't ignore the dire prognosis so I sent it off to my brother, Bill for his review. Just in case.

Now here I was, twelve days later, knowing that I needed to actually address the matter. I'd cleaned up some of the language and added corrected information. I wanted it to be perfect, something Mom might have read in the newspaper and remarked, "Isn't this nice."

We had the photo, one she chose herself. "This would make a good obituary picture," she said when providing the usual approval for any photo I took of her. I sent it to my brothers for review and we agreed with her choice.

So this was on my mind as I began today's unearthing task. My habit was to jump from one task to the next when I needed to reduce anxiety. I pulled over another bag and fished out an item

I grabbed from her bathroom. A make-up bag.

But this was no ordinary make-up bag. It was leather and had the image of four 1950-era smiling women in bathing suits splashing in the surf. We were in some store, on some trip, and she had delighted in it, and so, of course, she had to have it. Every trip demanded a remembrance, at the least, a magnet. Rather than actually take the chance of wearing it out, the bag sat on her bathroom shelves where she could delight in it every day.

Because I thought I might actually use the bag as a dear memento, I opened the zipper to look inside. I was surprised to find a number of unused toiletries but even more, a folded index card tucked in between the items.

Dated 10-12-2020, it said, "Dear Susan, Thank you for this beautiful bag, picturing memories of the 1950s! Love you always and forever, Mom." The word forever was underlined, and the exclamation point had a heart instead of a dot, which was a signature for her.

So apparently we bought it in 2020. And she decided to include a note that I would find once she was gone.

I returned to the most recent envelope before focusing again on the obituary. And a second sign appeared when I found two drafts she'd written twenty years earlier. They included the basics about what she wanted to include, like the fact that she and my father met in high school while performing in "Kiss Me Kate" where she had the lead. The name of the church where they were married. Details I would have missed otherwise.

Such a beautiful day of signs from Mom.

Sunday, 2/1 – Discovered a poem and many handwritten notes that she had penned over the years and tucked away.

Tuesday, 2/2 – I went into neutral, got in the car and headed to her apartment to begin the daunting job of organizing and cleaning. But when I opened the door to her place I became paralyzed, observing all her belongings so carefully displayed in front of me. There was her fake fireplace that she loved so much. A world she created out of little gnome characters that I found for her at the Family Dollar store, set up along the half-wall between the kitchen and the living room. A large display of mirrors in interesting frames. Walking from room to room I viewed her worldly possessions in an entirely new way.

Who would want these things? Panic was setting in and I had no idea where to begin.

Every time Mom would send something home with me, she would pack it in a hauling bag. The ones at TJ Maxx were her favorite. And so I had adopted this method of moving items because it was manageable. I placed my two overnight bags on her bed trying not to hyperventilate. When I got up, one of the bags fell on the floor. I hadn't bothered to read the image on the outside of the bag when I left home, but there was her message looking right back at me.

The saying? "You can do ANYTHING you put your mind to."

Instantly I felt better. I could do this. She had entrusted me to do this. I would not disappoint.

With a renewed attitude I drove to the funeral home for my 10:00 am appointment. She had chosen wisely. The building was only ten minutes from her home. The director could not have been more kind. He reviewed all the details she put in place and familiarized me with the plan. When I left, I felt composed. And when I returned to her place, I dropped my coat on the floor, locked the door, crawled into bed and spent the afternoon under the covers, her blankets tucked under my chin.

Wednesday, 2/3 – The night before I'd crawled out of bed around 4 pm and had begun sorting her belongings. I had no particular plan other than not to immediately throw anything away. It was almost midnight when my knees buckled as I got out of the kitchen chair and I realized that I couldn't summon another moment of being an adult.

I likened the process to a moving meditation. Choose a spot. Pick up whatever was in front of me. Bring it to the kitchen table. Go through the bags and envelopes piece by piece. Decide what to save and what to throw. Fill trash bag after trash bag. Save photos and mementos in bags labeled for each family member. Create bags for the homeless shelter.

I moved like an efficient robot but sleep did not come easy. I gave up any thought of actual rest and got up at 7 am. Headed into the bathroom. Mom didn't flush every time she used the toilet, and automatically I had done the same on Tuesday. So half asleep I flushed the few pieces of toilet paper left from Tuesday's visits.

You know that noise when the toilet is about to misbehave? When the water doesn't whoosh? I stood in disbelief as I watched the toilet bowl fill higher and higher and higher. Mom had told me that it occasionally acted up and how she threw down all her old towels to sop up the water only to find that it leaked through the ceiling in the downstairs apartment.

So I headed for the towels. And it kept coming. Now it was a fountain, spilling over the side in a steady stream. I still had to pee but had nowhere to go. Called and texted Mom's neighbor but she didn't answer. And so I told my brain to shut down that intense morning impulse, don't take a shower, throw on some clothes and pray.

I thought I'd lose my mind as the water refused to stop. I ran to the refrigerator and sure enough, there was the magnet with the number for emergency maintenance. Of course. Left a voicemail, got a call back, and 30 minutes went by before the plumber arrived.

As I stood in the bathroom doorway crying he assured me it would be all right. Once he replaced the fill valve and line, the toilet was in working order.

At first I didn't see this as a sign. But what if this had happened the morning of the funeral? And so I thanked Mom out loud for the timing.

Exhausted and distraught, I did what I could until almost Noon and then forced myself to stop. Hauled 12 bags of garbage to the dumpster. Assigned eight other bags to family members and four more bags for the homeless shelter. Back and forth I went with her trusty metal cart to the dumpster, an ergonomic wonder, and filled my car to the brim.

When I pulled out of her parking lot at 1:00 pm I was shaking from the effort of the prior 36 hours. I never looked so bad. Crying I asked Mom for a sign that it was going to all be okay. I turned the radio on and there it was. The first song was my absolute favorite of all time – *Maybe I'm Amazed* by Paul McCartney. The first line… "Maybe I'm amazed at the way you're with me all the time…" This was followed by The Byrds, *Turn, Turn, Turn*.

"To everything, turn, turn, turn,

There is a season, turn, turn, turn,

And a time to every purpose under heaven."

Reassurance that her love was around me as I navigated this necessary part of life.

Once on the interstate, two red tail hawks swooped right in front of my car. I knew I was being told to continue to pay attention to the signs.

Thursday, 2/4 – I could barely get out of my own way. Slept in two six-hour shifts, shell-shocked. But life goes on and I had to run errands which included picking up random household items at Family Dollar. When I walked in the door, at least fifty red mylar balloons in the shape of hearts greeted me. I know it was in preparation for Valentine's Day but the display felt like an *I Love You* reminder from Mom.

While driving, I began to think about handling a potentially volatile funeral situation. It is not uncommon for people who have wronged you in the past to come to your side when someone has died. I had those people in my life.

And so I thought of my mother who seemed to be able to move past any wrong with love in her heart. As I wrestled with the thought of them possibly attending the funeral, I waited for a sign.

"Tell me what to do," I said aloud. The message came once again through the radio, with Bobby Caldwell singing, *What You Won't Do, Do For Love*.

Friday, 2/5 – Mom's favorite colors were blue, purple and pink. I hadn't even thought about a casket spray until the funeral director reminded me. I visited the website of a local florist he recommended, typed in the search phrase, and there it was in Mom's exact three colors.

Twelve days had gone by and Mom had been guiding me every step of the way. I trusted she would continue to hold my hand, as I had begun to hold hers in mine over the past year when we walked together. I did not have to be afraid. In my grief and dismay, I knew she would help me to accept the inevitable with grace and gratitude.

IV. Concussion Psychosis

Gratefulness

Kind, wonderful children

Monthly income

No broken bones from fall

Nice apartment

Food and bed

Friends

None of the illnesses my neighbors have

My faith

Work on: Memories, walking, strength, eating better.

Mom's reminder list on her bedroom door

On July 6, 2021 I was at work when Mom's neighbor, Judy called. I knew this had to be bad news.

"Susan, this is Judy. I'm really sorry to tell you that the ambulance is taking Mom to the emergency room."

These are the calls that make you instantly alert, when your head detaches from your body. Although Judy wasn't sure exactly what had happened, she told me that she drove into the parking lot to see the ambulance loading a gurney. Behind the ambulance was a drainage grate, and she recognized Mom's blue leather shoe sticking upright in the metal dividers. Immediately she thought that Mom had been hit by a car and flew out of her shoe.

Judy went to her side as she awaited entry into the ambulance and learned that the toe of Mom's shoe had gotten stuck in the grate, causing her to fall forward on her left side. Her cheekbone smashed into the pavement and her head slammed down hard before all movement stopped.

"Her face is real bad, very swollen. She can't see out of her left eye and her cheek and forehead are cut. Could be more injuries but they don't know yet. I'm so sorry. I called Don so he could meet her at the hospital."

My breath stopped. I felt like I was underwater. My beautiful mother's face had taken the brunt of the fall. I imagined the worst of everything – broken bones, cuts needing stitches, eye injury. That's what happens when you're 88 and you take a bad fall. We all know about the dreaded broken hip.

Shortly after I hung up with Judy the phone rang. It was the EMT in the ambulance.

"I'm with your mother and she asked me to call to let you know what happened. It looks like she took a serious fall and her face is badly swollen and bruised. We're not sure about other injuries just yet but she is talking and able to answer questions. She even just told me every medication she is on and the dosage. It's pretty impressive. Her blood pressure and pulse are stable. But we are taking her to the trauma center at Hartford Hospital because the extent of her injuries need to be identified."

Mom had the presence of mind to remember my phone number so I could be notified and rattle off her medications to inform the technicians. Unbelievable.

I waited to hear from my brother, who arrived at her side soon thereafter. I asked him to take pictures to document the event. When he sent them to me, I screamed. It wasn't so much that her face was hideously swollen. It was that she was going to have to experience a great deal of pain and suffering before this would be behind her. To see her in the ER and clearly in fearful distress was hard to bear. And who knew just how bad it really was?

Her stay in the hospital lasted three days. Miraculously, and indeed every practitioner agreed that it was a true miracle, she did not break a single bone. No fractures but a dislocated left shoulder that prevented any movement, likely a rotator cuff injury. Her eye and vision was intact. Cheekbone and eye orbit bruised and swollen but not requiring any surgery. Forehead gash glued together to prevent a scar. The MRI did not show a brain bleed and she was told to watch out for potential symptoms.

No one could believe it. But she was down for the count. This recovery was going to take a long time, and she insisted she could live alone during the process. Judy, who had a career as a nurse, was there for her night and day, even going in after she was asleep to make sure she was still breathing. Home healthcare, physical and occupational therapy staff came and went. She could not drive or leave the house, and so my brother and Judy took care of getting her what she needed. When I visited her after she came home, I couldn't believe the view that greeted me. I dropped the flowers and presents I brought and held onto her and cried. The damage to her face was terrible.

That day she told me the details about what happened. One minute she was walking back from bringing a bag of trash to the dumpster. The next she was flying through the air as though being held by angels and laid as gently as possible on the ground, given the circumstance. Falling on her shoulder first, she said, broke the fall for her face and head. Not taking the brunt of the force on her hip prevented a break.

"It could have been so much worse," she kept saying, as though to minimize what she experienced. And that was true. It could have been. But what happened was horrid.

"The doctors really hurt me when they looked at my eye. They needed to pull apart the swelling so they could make sure my eye wasn't injured. When I was lying on the ground after I pushed my emergency button, blood was pouring everywhere down my face and I was afraid that my eye had popped out of the socket. So I bunched up my jacket and laid it under my head. When the ambulance got there, I kept asking them to make sure they picked up my eye. But it was still in place. So. That was good."

It was astonishing that she had the presence of mind to think clearly. I asked her if she knew how it happened. "The edge of the grate is uneven and the pavement is broken around it. I think there was a loose piece of cement that tripped me. My shoe must have caught on it and got stuck, and in seconds I was on the ground. Came right out of my shoe."

Her arm and shoulder were excruciatingly painful and the facial bruising extended down her neck and chest. She couldn't move her left arm. To say her quality of life changed in an instant is an understatement. Her cherished independence was now gone. She wasn't even well enough to lie outside on her chaise for an afternoon nap. Getting dressed, showering, typing on her keyboard, all were extremely difficult.

But worse than that was her melancholy. She was becoming more depressed by the hour. She said things like, 'I would have had five more good years left in me if this hadn't happened." She stopped eating because she had no appetite which caused a significant weight loss. Without food, she had no energy. Her world revolved around taking her meds, sitting in her electric recliner, watching tv and sending me a two sentence email when she used to write four times a day. She cried all the time.

By September she could move her arm somewhat, the worst of the facial swelling had subsided and the bruising turned various colors of purple, yellow and green. But now she had occasional headaches, something that never happened before. She was so disheartened.

Eventually the day came when she needed to get to the pharmacy and didn't want to ask anyone for help. Asserting her previous independence, she forced herself behind the wheel and drove two miles there and back.

"I know you told me not to drive yet, but I had to. And I'm sick of not doing anything. So I did it. I was really careful. I was scared, but I managed." I was amazed at her ability to plow forward, despite the circumstances. Yet she remained discouraged. Although she fell on her left side, it was her right hand that now shook with tremors. She could not work clasps, which required using two hands. Her prized penmanship was squiggly. It was hard for her to type.

Her 90th birthday was coming up in November and I was hoping for a recovery that would allow us to take our usual outings together. We'd missed the entire summer and a trip to the ocean.

"I'd really like to have one last trip to the ocean," she'd said to me. And so I planned it thoroughly, finding darling cottages in Wells, Maine where we could stay and take day trips to York, Ogunquit, Kennebunk and Old Orchard Beach. Neither of us had been to Old Orchard, and I was delighted to discover they had an operating ferris wheel and carousel. She adored merry-go-rounds. And ever mindful, those would make great photo ops.

She insisted on having her own space so I rented two tiny cottages for us for the week, side by side. They reminded her of the honeymoon tour she took with my father along the Cabot Trail. We were so looking forward to this trip as well as an overnight in Boston, where she could revisit trolley travel into the city with her mother and take a final ride on the swan boats in Boston Garden, their graceful plumage surrounding our seats as we glided on the lagoon. It was somehow reaffirming to know that the boats had remained in the founder's family since 1877 and that generations of mothers and daughters sat together on those wooden seats to gaze upon the surrounding beauty.

But then the accident happened and I had to cancel these final benchmarks. We planned to go in the summer of her 90th year instead. Best laid plans.

Her lucidity, which she prized, had also been impacted. "My thinking is fuzzy. I'm slower, not as sharp as I was." She was feeling as though her incredible run at life prior to the accident was now over. It was only when a case worker from the senior center came to visit her in August that he observed the problem.

"Jean, you've had a concussion. You can't help it. This is all part of the recovery which takes a long time."

When she told me what he said, I got online, and sure enough, all of her symptoms were indications of concussion psychosis, right down to the lack of appetite. Instantly she began to feel less downtrodden.

"It's not my fault, after all. It's because my brain needs to heal so the messages get through. I have to retrain it, like to have an appetite." Imagine her blaming herself for not doing a good enough job at recovery. I had no idea why none of the doctors who'd seen her had mentioned this critical information.

In September I tried some reverse encouragement that I knew would get her attention. "You know, if you can't actually recover from this terrible incident, then we might have to think about changing your living situation. I certainly don't mean a nursing home. But maybe you will need to move to Vermont after all, or

I will move to Connecticut and we'll live together."

The reaction I expected was immediate. "No, I need my own space and privacy. I'm fine here."

"But you're not. You won't eat. You've lost 25 pounds. You might think it's funny now that you now weigh what you did on your wedding day, but it's not helpful as you try to regain your life. And you are becoming weaker and weaker. I'm worried you're going to forget to take your meds. I worry about you all the time."

Rising to the threat to her independence, she replied, "Well, I could do better. My arm is improving a little, and I can drive to the doctors and grocery store. Just down the street. I will try harder to eat. And I could use my walker to go around the circle outside to get some exercise."

This persuasion had the desired effect. A warm September meant walks were pleasant, and she rediscovered napping outside in the afternoon, away from the television. Slowly she started to regroup, and her enthusiasm increased. Symptoms began to diminish with time, and she became encouraged about moving forward.

Our first outing since the accident was for her 90th birthday in November. We took a ride to revisit Gillette Castle, one of her favorite places filled with memories of our childhood family travels there. She managed to actually walk up 24 stone stairs to the very top in order to see the view of the Connecticut River from the mansion's outlook. We took it very slowly and I held her hand the entire way. I am grateful to have the sense memory of automatically holding her hand in mine, walking step by step as she would have once helped me.

After a fancy lunch we drove some back roads to get home, a glorious sunny fall day with the leaves in color on the trees. She exclaimed at the view and repeated her favorite phrase when she felt that the moment was perfect.

"I feel like I'm in a movie."

Although she still had a black bruise the size of a silver dollar indented in the middle of her cheek, her other physical injuries had begun to subside. Emotionally, she had suffered tremendously. The stress had taken a toll. Judy told me that she never dreamed Mom could come back to regain her life from the devastation in July. But we had high hopes for the coming year.

In the midst of it all, she remained grateful. Repeatedly she would tell me how much better off she was than so many of her neighbors, how it was a miracle she wasn't more seriously hurt, how fortunate she was to have the love of family and friends. Even a concussion couldn't keep her down.

But it did damage. And her earlier observation about no longer having another good five years was, apparently, a foreboding. When I packed up her apartment after she was gone and gathered her dress pants, I saw that she had placed six safety pins in the waist, three on each side, so they would fit.

Perhaps she thought they would one day fit her again when eating held its former joy. Or more likely she saw no reason to buy new pants when these were still perfectly good.

In hindsight, I believe that this traumatic event was the reason for Mom's death. Seven months after it, she was admitted to the

ICU and treated for an aortic hematoma, the long-term result of which is disproportionate bleeding.

The cause of her death was determined to be pericardial effusion, excess blood between the heart and the sac surrounding the heart. This medical condition can occur for a number of reasons, including blunt trauma resulting in injury to the heart from a car accident or a fall.

The very fact that she did not, incredibly, break any bones speaks to her otherwise good health. But the stress of working so hard to recover from her physical and emotional injuries, and the resulting concussion psychosis syndrome, proved to be too much. Ultimately, the intensity of her 90-year-old body hitting the pavement resulted in a hematoma that went undiagnosed.

By the time she was rushed to the trauma unit at Hartford Hospital on January 18, seven months later, irreversible damage to her heart had been done. She was robbed of those additional five years that awaited her, of her final trip to the ocean, of reliving her childhood joy seated on a swan boat.

Who was the thief? Nothing more dramatic than a lack of regular property maintenance.

V. Taking Care of Business

"One day your soul will carry you to the Beloved.
Don't get lost in your pain,
know that one day your pain will become your cure."

"Don't grieve. Anything you lose comes round in another form."

"The wound is the place where the light enters you."

"Whoever finds love beneath hurt and grief
disappears into emptiness with a thousand new disguises."

"What goes comes back. Come back.
We never left each other."

"Dance, when you're broken open.
Dance, if you've torn the bandage off.
Dance in the middle of the fighting.
Dance in your blood.
Dance, when you're perfectly free."

"Your body is away from me,
but there is a window open
from my heart to yours."

"But listen to me:
for one moment, quit being sad.
Hear blessings dropping their blossoms around you."

"What hurts you, blesses you.
Darkness is your candle."

> "Goodbyes are only for those who love with their eyes.
> Because for those who love with heart and soul
> there is no such thing as separation."
>
> "Grief can be the garden of compassion.
> If you keep your heart open through everything,
> your pain can become your greatest ally in your life's search for
> love and wisdom."
>
> *RUMI*

No-one tells you how hard it will be. That there is simply no way to integrate the process of grieving someone you loved while being responsible for their end-of-life necessities. You must walk both paths simultaneously, one foot in each world, or alternatively abdicate the task entirely by turning it over to the funeral home and lawyers.

This would not do for my mother. Her very specific instructions were meant to make the final goodbye as personal as possible. She drafted obituaries, jotted down many hymn lists, chose her goodbye photo and outfit. She knew what she wanted and she expected me to follow through. Abdication was never an option.

Nor did I want to be absent during this sacred time. I quit my job because I could not manage this full-time responsibility and also sit at my desk. My brain could not possibly care about the content of my mother's obituary and work with any of the seven computer platforms that required my input each day. I needed the most flexibility possible for review of my to-do list while trying to recover from the trauma of those final 18 minutes and accomplish whatever rose to the surface. There was such satisfaction in crossing off yet another task that honored her life.

Most of all I needed time, time to stop at any point, crawl under the covers, distract myself with foreign language crime dramas and, of course, cry. Weeping was unpredictable. As was ugly crying. I didn't care what I looked like when I had to go out. In many ways it was incredibly freeing. My universe had been isolated and confined to me and my mother. The way it was when I first entered this world.

Organizing her earthly belongings was a huge task. She made me promise to go through every clasp envelope to retrieve what was valuable rather than automatically make a decision to toss it. I had to handle every photo album, every cherished furnishing, gifts from all of us over her lifetime. She kept her past firmly rooted in the present with photos taped on doors, doorways, kitchen cabinets. They were stuck in the corners of framed photos, held on the refrigerator with magnets. It gave her tremendous joy to see these images each day, all day.

I must have opened 100 large brown kraft envelopes. Instructions were written on the front of them. *Important Papers! Super Important Advice! Medical Solutions! Old-Fashioned Remedies! Save – Vintage Recipes! Exercises To Do NOW! Do Not Throw Away!*

My favorites were the remedies. Newspaper and magazine clippings going back decades held the promise of cures for arthritis, leg cramps, headaches, sinus problems, tooth and gum relief, gout, pain of all kinds and itching. She was very big on itching solutions and discovered the magic of white vinegar as the antidote to itches that just otherwise could not be scratched. The gallon in her cupboard was proof that she was serious about this.

One arthritis remedy she never tried but recommended to others was gin-soaked raisins. I contemplated buying gin for the sole purpose of creating this magic potion but never did. Not that she would have actually eaten them. A sip of prosecco on special occasions was as far as she got with alcohol.

And cherries for gout. For a while she bought heavy glass bottles of cherry juice at Ocean State Job Lots. She did not have gout, but wanted to make sure she avoided this possibility. There was a year when I'd haul three of them home with me after each visit.

Making decisions about what to pass along was straightforward. Pictures would be returned to each family member represented in them. Some items had recipient names already attached to them. She told me what she wanted to go to her grandchildren. I focused on the low-hanging fruit with the initial pass.

A big stumbling block was the genealogical information she had painstakingly compiled. Her sister had begun gathering their family details and those records had been passed along to my mother, which she had continued to enhance. In the process she also collected my father's family history. I found it incredibly intriguing to read Ellis Island records of both branches, a complete story of how we got here over the last 150 years. Birth certificates. Death certificates. Stoic unknown relatives standing side by side.

She pored over each line, each faded photo, getting to know the men and women who came before. A near obsession with the death of a brother, Baby Francis, who burned his hand on the stove causing septicemia, haunted her. He was only 2 years old and his wake was held in the house. She recalled hearing her mother in the living room, rocking back and forth as she wept. Was this the reason that Nana Kay never seemed to regain happiness in her life? And the reason my mother had no recollection of ever being held or kissed by her mother?

Her repeated worry to me was that no-one would want the information when she was gone. What was invaluable to her would only be a nuisance to us. I was able to confirm with a cousin, the son of her brother, that her MacKay birth family archives would go to him. But my oldest brother was dealing with his own family suffering and could not undertake this task for my father's family. Brother Don agreed to safeguard the archives for another day.

I had already brought home 12 bags of items that were stacked in my living room to go through. It was what remained after tossing out an additional 12 bags of trash.

And I wasn't done yet. Her spare bedroom had become the computer room. Boxes that had been packed pre-pandemic, when the plan was for her to move to Vermont to be near me, sat stacked neatly against the wall. Floor to ceiling. And no identification of what was in each one. Those would be the last to handle before St. Vincent DePaul came by to pick up the remaining furniture.

As a Catholic who went to church in the 50s and 60s, you probably heard of St. Vincent DePaul. My mother would roll the five syllables off her tongue as though it was one word... saintvincentdepaul. I remember wondering why I never heard of this saint in my weekly Sunday School classes. Some masses would include a special envelope for a donation to the mystery group, and these would drop into the collection basket along with the weekly tithe.

Although I never really knew the purpose of the organization, I was delighted to discover that in the 21st century it still existed to help others. And that you could arrange for volunteers to come to your house and pick up furniture you wished to donate, which would then be given to those in need. This would have made my devout mother very happy.

Her many personal belongings and clothing were disbursed to my brother's church and to the local Savers store which took in unwanted items and priced them to sell. She loved going to Savers and found many incredible buys, but her favorites were fancy Vera Bradley purses, wallets and carry-on bags. The purses suited her well since they were roomy and could be washed. And it didn't hurt that they would be recognizable to most women as designer bags. No one had to know she only paid $5 at Savers. Mom loved a bargain.

Thinking about all the discarded items at Savers made me wonder how they arrived on the store's doorstep. Originally I'd thought of the place as the repository where someone could bring what was left after cleaning out their closet. But this is very different than realizing many of the items, like my mother's, were what was left behind after a life was gone. I imagined the decisions that had been made, just like my own, about what to move along and what to discard. Were those fancy Vera Bradley households any different than my mother's in the end?

VI. On Becoming a Motherless Child

"Motherless Child," African American Spiritual, 1870s

The song is an expression of pain and despair as it conveys the hopelessness of a child who has been torn from his or her parents.

"As Harriet Jacobs, an escaped slave, wrote: "On one of those sale days, I saw a mother lead seven children to the auction block. She knew that some of them would be taken from her; but they took all. The children were sold to a slave-trader, and their mother was bought by a man in her own town. Before night her children were all far away. She begged the trader to tell her where he intended to take them; this he refused to do."

—from The Classic Slave Narratives, edited by Henry Louis Gates, Jr.

Death is the ultimate demarcation line from which there is no return for a child and a parent. One minute you are irrevocably attached to a loved one and the next, the tether is gone. I imagine the desolation of losing a child is similar to losing a parent, especially a mother, because in both cases the symbiotic connection once provided the very meaning of life.

As Mom aged I became more devoted to her. Although I always made sure to shower her with gifts and provide opportunities for us to be connected, once she reached 80 I became excruciatingly aware that her time with me, her child, would be coming to an end.

I used to contemplate this fact on the two-hour drive to see her and it would inevitably bring tears. I'd find that the more I tried to ignore the thought of her dying, the more my thoughts conjured up scenario after scenario to preoccupy my imagination. At first it felt selfish and narcissistic to become stuck in this pretense, and then fearful as the crescendo built and I realized that I might actually be creating her death by 'thinking it into existence.'

Anxiously, I'd erase any thought of her eventual demise and instead send a prayer to the heavens that her final ending needed to be a loooong way away. But images of a torn mother-child bond would float in my consciousness until I'd purposely tie each end into a bow.

It's amazing how adrift I felt while sitting at her bedside after she died. Not only did the shell on the bed no longer resemble my beautiful mother but it was literally empty. As I took her hand I wondered if it would crumble within my grasp. There was no sense of humanity. No heart. No soul. No emotion. The reciprocity I had always cherished from my mother was simply gone.

And that was the moment it hit me. I no longer had a mother. I could look to her friends for solace, serving as a substitute in my moment of need. My own friends were absolutely by my side to do whatever I asked. And I had my mother's evocative reminiscences to call upon when the emptiness rose up.

But then another reality shocked my senses; my behavior toward my mother was the end of a generational experience. Growing up in the 50s, 60s and 70s, I was witness to how my mother deferentially treated my grandmother, who at 72 looked ancient to me and never considered driving a car. My father would make the round-trip drive to Massachusetts to pick her up for a week-long stay, and her visit consisted of not much more than sitting in the rocking chair, thick stockings visible, sturdy black tie shoes with a chunky heel, stylish Jordan Marsh house dress reaching below her crossed knees. Her tightly permed hair never looked any different, as though it was a wig. The television was inevitably droning on in the background. How she considered rocking and watching tv in my mother's house as a vacation get-away was beyond me.

There was never a question that the drive was part of the responsibility, an obligation willingly fulfilled. And so when highway nerves began to worry my mother she curtailed long drives from Connecticut to New Hampshire and Vermont. It was therefore natural for me to simply get in the car to visit, creating special day or weekend trips where I would add another 90 minutes or two hours just to reach our destination. I'd end up driving eight hours before I returned home, exhausted but satisfied that my labor of love was complete.

Me at 68 was a far cry from my grandmother at that age. My mother was still confident and energetic at 68, but not youthful as I am now. Once she turned 85, and I began to hold her hand more frequently, either crossing the street or just walking together, I was aware we were passing a threshold. There was never a discussion about it. She just reached over, and I naturally enfolded her hand in mine.

The shock was realizing that likely no one would do this for me. On one hand, I recognized that my independence meant that others didn't have to worry about me. My son would not even think of holding my hand when we were together. On the other, this realization made me bereft. It meant I alone was responsible for myself.

My granddaughter, Kiyah, is very close to me. When she's home, we go to our favorite restaurant where she enjoys the Big Sexy cocktail and we don't think twice about what we're going to order because it's always the same favorite appetizers. It's just what we do. And I love that ease with her.

After Mom died and Kiyah and I were together for the first time, she did surprise me by reaching for my hand. She had never done this before. In fact, she and I never discussed my holding Mom's hand. But I think she knew how vulnerable I was feeling, and so in a very take-charge way she led me by the hand, down the sidewalk, through the door of the restaurant, only letting go as we got in single file to be led to our table. I resonated with this natural feeling of continuity.

At that moment I recalled our 2003 school vacation trip to Florida. Kiyah was 9-years-old and Disney beckoned. We were in the pool on a cloudy morning before heading out for the day. "Hold me like a baby, Nana," she asked. I gathered her in my arms, recalling when she measured elbow to elbow in the crook of my embrace.

"You are so big, look at you!" I let her drop down into the water so that my arms cradled her shoulders and knees. I walked with her, weightless, in the shallow end. Slowly, I rocked from side to side, feeling the resistance of the water.

"Push, me, Nana. Push me against the will of water."

The will of water. I marveled at her language. "Where did you hear that, the will of water?"

"I don't know," she replied with a shrug. "I just made it up. The water has a mind of its own. The will of water.'

I whirled her around and around in circles while she squealed with delight, and then let go as she sliced through the crest of our turbulence, confident that I would not let her sink. Just as she would now do the same for me.

A mother's love is like the will of water, a formidable force. A mother's embrace is trustworthy. A mother's devotion will keep you afloat even when her body transcends space and time.

But now the one person whose hand I had most enjoyed holding was gone. Her smile would no longer light up a room. Every time I walked in the door it was clear that no one would ever love me like she loved me. Her eyes held the joy of moments past and the hours to come when we would be together. Her arms would reach out toward me with enthusiasm and no matter what I thought of my appearance on any given day she would always say, "You look beautiful!" And she meant it.

She loved it when my long hair reappeared after decades of absence, thanks to the pandemic. She would always compliment my nails, my skin, the color of my eyes. And she was proud of me, my artwork on display front and center in her living room.

When I cleaned out her apartment I discovered that she had saved everything, from my childhood cards and paintings to published articles by me and about me. Benchmarks of my life. Finding this memorabilia made me wonder if I ever thanked her enough for the love and devotion she poured into my being. If I spent enough time with her so she knew that she was front and center in my life.

I am haunted by not knowing the answers to these questions now that it's too late.

I pray that I did enough.

The Final Descent

It's official. I have become a motherless child.

The tether is gone, and I am adrift, yowling in the night like the abandoned cat outside my window.

Seeking a familiar touch, missing the daily emails, Facebook hearts, phone calls, cards that say I love you.

No longer listening to her sing along with Rosemary Clooney as we head out on another mystery ride. "Now this is real music. You could dance to this music. You could fall in love to this music."

Calling from her hospital bed. "Honey, I'm so sorry to have to tell you this, but I think I'm dying."

Spending the final 18 minutes of her earthly existence on the phone with her.

Sorting through 90 years of life. Three suitcases full of cards from everyone who loved her. Poems and stories in beautiful penmanship, flowing cursive expressions of gratitude and love. Love notes planned well in advance, awaiting my discovery.

A million photos. Fascination with stern men and women of good Scottish stock whose 1800s lives would have been forgotten but for her tending.

Ever the diligent pupil, I served as the arbiter of what to keep, to pass along, to discard. She insisted I attend When Mom Dies School, even though her thoughtful instruction made me cry.

Our final outing was a New Year's Eve luncheon. She closed her eyes on the ride home, something she never did, as Rosemary sang her to sleep. 18 days later she began the final descent.

Sweet Dreams, Mom.

VII. The Birthday Book

"Today you are You; that is truer than true.

There is no one alive who is Youer than You."

– Dr. Seuss

There was a time when cards and letters were sent through the mail. Handwritten missives in fine cursive writing were anticipated gifts, almost more important than any tangible object. Early postcards from the 19th and 20th century were works of art and featured delicate embossed pansies, bluebells, roses, lace and pastoral scenes.

My mother kept every card she ever received. When she moved ten years ago she had three suitcases full, so at that time they covered 70 years of her life. We discussed how much she loved them and likely how much others would not care to keep them once she was gone. But to her they were proof of family, connection, and most of all, love. There was no consideration of parting with a single one.

And she didn't just cherish her own cards. She also loved to collect vintage postcards. They covered the usual holidays, but she focused especially on the birthday messages. Each one was a work of art on 3x5 cardstock, covered in floral happiness with raised images. They come alive in your hand and it's easy to imagine someone choosing just the right one with great care to reflect the intention of the greetings, some with language as floral as the design.

Birthday Greetings, I Wish Thee Many Happy Birthdays

Fond Birthday Wishes, That You'll Remember Me

May Birthday Greetings Hearty and True, Bring Peace and Happiness To You

For Your Birthday, I'd like to send a Birthday gift, To show you my regard; But it could bring no greater love, Than this small postal card

As each rose that doth unfold, Seemeth fairer than the last, So may every Birthday hold, Something sweeter than the past

Hearty Wishes for your Birthday, The Birthdays Come, And the Birthdays go, The question is — where do they find us, Have we learned to laugh At the ills of life And leave dull care behind us? Have we learned to make each passing day Yield all the Good that's in it? If not, it's time we should turn around And begin right away THIS MINUTE.

Birthday Greetings, A loving wish for Birthday bright, Filled with gladness and delight.

Postcards were the quick version of letters. Some of the cards she gave to me are blank on the back, while others have personal messages inscribed in the small space.

"Dear Mrs. E, Will write later. Got home yesterday. Am going to Pittsfield Sat. to see a sick lodge member. Yours Truly, F.R.D."

"Dear Ruth, How are you getting along with your birthday? Hope you are getting along fine and having a good time. I have the meeting next Wed. They elect officers. Hear ministers and preachers next Sunday. Come up. Mary."

"Dear Mr. Seaman, A little bird told me in whispering song that on March the 15th you'll be 80 yrs. Young. I think that is making a very good start. May blessings go with you is the wish of my heart. Nelly Ruth Cramers."

But what I held most dear was when she would write and date a message to me on the back of the postcard. Often they would be tucked inside my Hallmark birthday card. As a greeting card fanatic, Mom commemorated every occasion – birthdays, holidays, anniversaries, happiness, sorrow, graduations, baptisms, weddings. No card would be sent without a personal note from her. And every address from the last 50 years was a sacred entry in The Birthday Book.

Well, let me clarify. There wasn't just one Birthday Book. There were three, each in varying states of falling apart. They sat in the middle of a large round tin on her kitchen table, right next to pens and stamps and return address stickers. At some point in the last ten years she discovered that the Hallmark store could provide two necessities. One was a calendar that had a pocket on the bottom for bills or any other important papers. The other was an oversize address book of the same design. Her monthly visit to the card mecca would result in her spending hours, and I do mean hours, to find exactly the right card with the right words. She wasn't just sending cards. She was sending keepsakes.

Those cards would end up in the monthly pocket awaiting their mailing date, which also included a daily calendar. Each name was written on the corresponding date line with an indication of the occasion – birthday, anniversary, etc. Then when the card was sent, she would note the year beside the name so she would know at a glance that her wishes had been mailed. It was unacceptable to forget anyone.

Knowing how much she loved cards I began sending her weeks of cards before each occasion. For instance, I'd buy six cards for her birthday or Valentine's Day or Mother's Day and send one each week leading up to the big day. During the first six months of the pandemic in 2020, I sent her a card every week. She loved putting them up on every flat surface in her home, and when she ran out of room they would be taped on the doors and kitchen cabinets. It was her way of being surrounded by love that included a daily practice of reading each one.

Although I knew the Birthday Book existed, I did not pay that much attention other than to admire her consistent, loving practice. That is, until the last 18 minutes of her life, when she entrusted me with its importance. Because when she told me that it was now my job to take on this remembrance journey, I knew that she knew her life was at an end. To be so lucid as to tell me which Valentine's Day card was specifically for Auri, chosen because Mom knew it would make her laugh, was an extraordinary testament to how much she loved every single person who would never receive a card from her again.

When I returned to her apartment after she was gone, and stood in the kitchen, the first thing I grabbed were all three address books. I had been entrusted with her legacy and I considered it more important than any other task I would undertake.

Two days after she died I sat at my own kitchen table, as she did, and placed the books in front of me. I began with the most tattered version, reliving decades of people who had come and gone, new addresses scratched over old ones, including my own. She had taped business cards here and there, and return addresses that had been on envelopes. By the time I reached the pockets of the newer book I was shattered.

The next day I stood in the card aisle and looked at the list of cards that still needed to be purchased according to her records. I spent time honoring her memory by carefully choosing which cards she would want to send. Dutifully I included a sticky note inside each card I prepared indicating that I was signing on behalf of Mom, at her request.

The real difficulty came when I was cleaning out her apartment. She had whittled down three suitcases of cards to one. Inside, the cards were organized in elastics, tied ribbon, twine. "From Charlie, From Mom, From Marie, From Susan, From Bill, From Don, From Bruce."

But the cards didn't stop there. A floor to ceiling wall of packed boxes and large tubs included, among many items, more clasp envelopes filled with cards. *Special Cards. Do Not Throw Away These Cards! Keep Cards from Dad to Me.* The cards told the story of Hallmark and family through the decades. I found myself in angst as I opened each large envelope to discover what was inside. Some I could part with but so many others I just couldn't.

And that is why I have 15 large carry bags in my apartment waiting for me to unearth and distribute what is inside, including mementos with my name taped on them, ones that I was seeing for the first time. Like religious medals that belonged to my grandmother's two sisters who were nuns. Sister Beatrice I met and remember. She sent me an alpaca shawl from Brazil and a wooden music box. I never met Sister Andrea but knew she was a child prodigy at the piano. And now I have her Patsyette doll from 1926.

What will I ever do with these things? Nothing. They are mine to treasure.

When I'm gone will anyone care? Probably not.

But I just can't part with them. Because Mom gave them to me. Her hands held each piece, wrote each note, gathered up each tin and box filled with her wishes.

And so much love.

VIII. Visiting Hours

REMEMBER

Remember

when it's time for me to go.

Remember

how much I loved you.

Remember

if I did anything that made you happy

that you, the very act of your being alive,

gave me every minute of the sweetest joy.

Remember

if I ever did anything that caused you hurt or pain,

I am so very sorry.

Remember

all the times you visited me, or we talked on the phone.

Remember

all the sweet gifts of time and thoughtfulness,

18 Minutes

and all the cards.

Remember

your patience when I took your pictures

as they gave me endless pleasure.

Remember.

-Jean A. Brady

The phrase 'visiting hours' conjures up nerve-wracking hospital encounters, where medical staff have control over whether or not you can see your loved one as they lay in their uncomfortable adjustable bed feeling afraid and alone.

This is a necessary cruelty, I suppose, which became even more onerous when the pandemic struck. I can't even imagine what it must have been like for patients with Covid and their family members unable to be in each other's presence as they suffered and died. What a horrendous reality, a memory that will haunt both the living and the dead.

So being able to see Mom within the visiting parameters of one visitor per day for 20 minutes felt like a tremendous blessing. And as I watched the clock tick well beyond the allotted 20 minutes I felt like a kid stealing a candy bar, deliberately not meeting the eyes of observant staff while beaming out an energy that indicated I was refusing to adhere to the rules. My plan was to get away with what I could while Mom was hospitalized, and it worked.

Yet what struck me was that our bedside conversation focused on all the prior visiting hours that weren't constrained by beeping medical equipment and flashing digital numbers. Endless trips we took, the fun we had, the unexpected travel opportunities. The lobster rolls ... so many lobster rolls and restaurant meals and keepsakes from every trip to "remember the day."

Adventures were chronicled in a mountain of photos for us both. Mom liked to remind me that she was grateful for all the time we spent together and the adventures we enjoyed, and if I ever forgot I should just look at the pictures "to prove it."

Now that she's gone, I have an entirely new point of view about visiting hours. We should think of every chance to be together with someone we love as the ultimate visiting hours that celebrate life, not the scary visiting hours that make your heart beat quickly and cause shortness of breath as you fear the bad news while keeping your fingers crossed for something, anything good.

Cherish the daily visiting hours. Make sure to create time in your life for that special trip or event. Understand as it is happening that the moment will be gone in a flash, so take lots of pictures, even if this means your executor will eventually have a very hard time figuring out what to do with them all. Because each image reflects the joy of the moment, heart touching heart, unbridled love and pride.

Most of all, remember the unexpected conversation, look, touch, and laughter. My favorite memories involve riding in the car, playing the Rosemary Clooney Pandora radio station so Mom could relive her youth. She'd sing along, marvel at how she remembered the words and regale me with her memories.

"Once when it was late and we were coming back from going out, Daddy and I went to the tennis court across the street from my house and danced together under the moon. This was real music. Beautiful songs you could dance to. Romantic. It's gone now, but I lived it, and I'm glad I did."

And then there was the "lady in the radio," otherwise known as my Waze GPS. While we navigated our way to parts unknown, we depended upon this authoritative voice to tell us everything we needed to know.

"Watch out. Pothole ahead. Vehicle on side of road. Turn left, then turn right. In 1.3 miles, take the next exit."

Sometimes Mom would hold my phone to watch the progress of our vehicle en route, mesmerized by the fact that this technology even existed. As the arrow moved she would become increasingly alert. And if the lady was slow to provide all-important directions, a sound scolding would follow.

"Wake up!" Mom would command. "You're not on break! Tell us what to do next! You need to improve your job performance, or you will be fired!"

She would lean into the phone held in her hand or toward the center console where it sat to deliver this missive. The ongoing conversation was hysterically funny for us both, and the more I laughed, the more Mom persisted in chatting with the unseen, all-knowing lady. It felt like I was a toddler, and my mother had discovered something special to delight me.

These are the beautiful, gut-wrenching moments that I will always recall. When the lady in the radio talks to me now, without her, I smile through my tears.

IX. Good Morning and Good Night

Prayer for Now

Normal day, let me be aware of the treasure you are. Let me learn from you, love you, savor you, bless you before you depart. Let me not pass you by in quest of some rare and perfect tomorrow. Let me hold you while I may, for it will not always be so. One day I shall dig my nails into the earth, or bury my face in the pillow, or stretch myself taut, or raise my hands to the sky, and want more than all the world your return.

-Mary Jean Irion

I miss the daily emails and phone calls. Morning, noon, night. Jumping onto email first thing as the day began and last thing as the day ended to make sure I'd heard from her. I could read between the lines if anything was off. If her name did not appear in my inbox, I'd be on the phone. And if she didn't answer, the next line of defense was to call neighbor Judy. Because Mom was always thinking of me, wanting to share her hourly story, her words were an electronic umbilical cord linking me to her heart and soul.

Now there is only emptiness and pain each day when I open my email and know that she will not be there.

The same was true of her voicemails.

"You don't have to call me back. I just wanted to share a nice thing that happened to me."

"I'm not sure if you saw the weather for today, but it looks like we are going to get heavy rain. Do you have good tires so you don't hydroplane?"

"It's going to be very cold today, so be sure you have what you need in your car in case of an emergency. Water. Crackers. Warm hat. Blanket. Flashlight."

She was my mother, and I was her child. It didn't matter that I was 68 years old.

Every email was signed the same way, with anywhere from three to six 'o's' in the word, Love. As previously mentioned, this was the result of a mistake she once made and we both liked it so much that it became our signature goodbye, mine and hers. The four letters that comprised the endearment simply weren't enough.

The more o's, the more love.

Below are some of her last emails to me, always in capital letters. She was constantly fearful of winter weather, a surefire disaster just waiting to happen for either her or me.

When I'd told her that the walkway into my building at work was very icy, she wrote:

-DEAR SUSAN, I AM HORRIFIED YOU ARE CRAWLING UP AND DOWN YOUR HILL. WHERE IS MAINTENANCE? CAN YOU CALL THEM? THIS IS WAY TOO DANGEROUS TO BE DOING. CAN YOU USE ANOTHER ENTRANCE AND WALK THRU THE BUILDING? WILL BE GLAD WHEN REGISTRATION IS OVER. BUT WHY

HAVE IT IN THE MIDDLE OF THE WINTER IN VERMONT? SO I AM UP LATE. GOT A BEAUTIFUL CARD AND LETTER FROM A STUDENT I HAD IN CCD. THE ONLY ONE WHO KEPT IN TOUCH. SHE WILL GRADUATE FROM BU THIS MAY. SO NOW TO GET DRESSED. OH SHOOT PLEASE BE CAREFUL GETTING INTO WORK AND INTO THE CAR. FOREVER LOVE AND HUGS, LOOOOVE, MOM

Black ice was one of her greatest fears.

–DEAR SUSAN. –SO THE BOTTOM HALF OF MY RAMP IS PURE ICE. I USED THE REST OF MY ICE MELT BUT IT DIDN'T WORK. –JUDY GETTING SAND FROM BELOW WHEN SHE GETS THE MAIL AND WILL PUT IT ON. I ALSO USED HALF A BOX OF SALT AND THAT SEEMED TO HELP JUST NOW. BLACK ICE AS YOU CAN'T SEE IT. BUT I AM A PRISONER FOR NOW. REMEMBER THE SALT THO AS A LAST RESORT. WE ARE TOLD SOME SNOW THURSDAY AND A LOT ON SATURDAY. I THINK I WENT THRU EVERY PAPER IN THE KITCHEN, WILL START THE BEDROOM PAPERS TOMORROW.. HOW IS YOUR DAY GOING? WHAT IF IT STORMS ON THURSDAY FOR WORK? BYE FOR NOW AND FOREVER LOVE, LOOOVE, MOM

Every day, another list to accomplish. And weather.

-DEAR SUSAN, FINISHED A FEW THINGS OFF THE LIST. MADE THE REST OF THE BATCH OF OATMEAL COOKIES AND GAVE JUDY SOME. MY BIG

CONCERN FOR YOU IS BIG TIME ICE TOMORROW MORNING. SO GOING TO BED SOON. OUR RAIN STOPPED AND NOW JUST WET READY TO FREEZE A.M. LIFE IS DIFFICULT BEYOND WORDS. I CANNOT BELIEVE IT, IT'S SNOWING AGAIN AT 7:30 P.M.☐☐☐☐ FOREVER LOVE AND HUGS, LOOOVE, MOM

Attending church in her chair. And weather.

-DEAR SUSAN, WAS UP AT 4 AND SAW THE 5 A.M. MASS. CAN'T BELIEVE THEY DELIVERED THE PAPER IN THIS TEMP. TV SAYS 80 MILLION PEOPLE IN THE EYE OF THE STORM. I CAN'T EVEN COMPREHEND 80 MILLION PEOPLE. SO YOU ARE GOING OUT TODAY IN MINUS DEGREES WEATHER. NECESSARY BUT PLEASE BE AWARE EVERY MINUTE. I NEED TO GET DRESSED. HAPPY NEW DAY. FOREVER LOVE AND HUGS, LOOOVE, MOM

Danger always lurked on a winter's day, yet it was met with a plan.

-DEAR SUSAN, UP AND DRESSED AND COFFEED. VERY COLD AIR PLUS WINDY. WILL WORK ON THE BEDROOM, DID THE FIRST LAYER, NOW TO ATTACK THE SECOND. KEEP A SET OF WARM STUFF IN YOUR CAR LIKE A WARM HAT AND GLOVES, A BLANKET, WATER AND SNACKS. IN CASE YOU GET STUCK IN TRAFFIC. I KNOW IT SEEMS LIKE OVERDOING BUT CAN BE LIFE SAVING IN A SITUATION LIKE VIRGINIA. OKAY, KEEP ME POSTED. STAYING IN ALL DAY. MORE LOOOOVE, MOM

—DEAR SUSAN, SO CHECKED AT 2 A.M. AND BIG SNOW STORM. AT 6 A.M. DRENCHING RAIN AND WIND. 4000 WITHOUT POWER. SNOW IN OTHER PARTS OF CT. STILL DARK AND BIG TIME RAIN. AT LEAST GETTING RID OF THE SNOW. WE ARE TOLD PURE ICE ON EVERYTHING TOMORROW MORNING. SO NOW TO GET DRESSED. HAVE A GOOD DAY OF REST AND BAKING. BACK LATER AND FOREVER LOVE AND HUGS, LOOOOVE, MOM

—DEAR SUSAN. LOOKING LIKE 6 INCHES ON THE PATIO TABLE. PRETTIEST THING IS THE LIGHTS ON THE FENCE SHINING THRU THE SNOW. SO GLAD YOU ARE INSIDE. BE SUPER CAREFUL OPENING THE ICE MELT. TERRIBLE JOB THEY DID MAKING IT CHILD PROOF. I USED THE TIP OF A STEAK KNIFE TO BEND UP AND BREAK THE TAB. DRESSED AND NOW FOR SOME FOOD. FOREVER LOVE YOU, LOOOVE, MOM

—DEAR SUSAN, YOUR MOTHER SAID TO ASK YOU NOT TO GO OUT TODAY BECAUSE IT IS MINUS 1 DEGREES. WAY TOO DANGEROUS, AND JUST TO STAY HOME. NOT WORTH TAKING A CHANCE. 5:30 AND SHE IS UP FOR THE DAY. ALSO SNOW ON MONDAY. AND WEDNESDAY. UGH! SHE SENDS YOU FOREVER LOVE AND HUGS AND LOOOVE, HER OTHER SELF

—OUR NEWS SAYING ALSO DANGER OF FROSTBITE AND HYPOTHERMIA. OUR SNOW STARTS AT MID-

NIGHT. GOING BACK TO BED FOR AWHILE. SUPER LOOOOVE, XXOO

-DEAR SUSAN, OUR WEATHERMAN JUST SAID CT. IS AN ICE NIGHTMARE WITH MULTIPLE ACCIDENTS. I IMAGINE VT. IS NO DIFFERENT. YOUR STAIRS, WALKWAYS STREET ETC ARE TREACHEROUS. I DON'T HAVE A GREAT REACTION TO THE SHOT. JUST SOMEWHAT, NOT TOO BAD. SO BLESSED I CAN REST ALL DAY. HOPING YOU MAKE CAREFUL DECISIONS FOR TRAVELING THIS WEEK. KEEP ME POSTED. FOREVER LOVE AND HUGS. BYE FOR NOW AND MORE LOOOOOOOOVE, MOM

And when the weather wasn't her biggest worry, she was celebrating daily gratitude and my accomplishments.

-DEAR SUSAN, JUST ATE ONE OF YOUR BLUEBERRY MUFFINS RIGHT OFF THE PAGE .... THEY LOOK WONDERFUL ..... THE PINK SKY MIDDLE PAINTING IS SO REAL IT LOOKS LIKE A PHOTO..... ESPECIALLY WITH THE GREENERY ON THE CORNER, SO YOU ARE LOOKING UP AT THE SKY. I HAD 6 BIG SHRIMP FOR LUNCH WITH NOODLES. LOVE YOU HAVE THE DAY TO BAKE AND PAINT! NOW I HAVE TO DO SOMETHING USEFUL. FOREVER LOVE AND HUGS, LOOOVE, MOM

Nightly reminder that she treasured and loved me.

-DEAR SUSAN, GOING TO BED SOON. YOU PUT IN A VERY LONG DAY. A DAY OF GOODNESS AND CARING.

HOPE YOU SLEEP WELL. FOREVER LOVE AND HUGS, LOOOVE, MOM

Always looking forward while enjoying sweets. (And weather.)

-DEAR SUSAN, JUST WASHED OFF THE OLD YEAR WITH A HOT SHOWER AND WASHED MY HAIR. ALL DRESSED AND HAD THE REST OF THE POT PIE WHICH WAS A GOOD AMOUNT, AND THE BURNT SUGAR MUFFIN WITH COFFEE ICE CREAM. NO ONE ELSE CAN MATCH THAT BREAKFAST. GOING TO BE 53 HERE WITH RAIN TODAY AND 34 ON MONDAY. GOING TO MAKE MY BED AND PUT ON THAT BEAUTIFUL THROW ON TOP. LOOKING FORWARD TO THE DAY. MORE FOREVER LOVE AND GRATITUDE. LOOOVE, MOM

P.S. I AM SO GLAD WE EACH HAVE A CARDINAL FROM THE SHOP. IT IS WELL MADE AND A GREAT SOUVENEIR AND MEMORY. ALSO PUT A MAGNET FOR YOU IN THE BAG IN CASE YOU DIDN'T SEE I AND IT COULD BE THROWN AWAY. XXXXXOOOO

Endless computer challenges.

-DEAR SUSAN, SO IT HAPPENED AGAIN. I HIT GOOGLE AND THEN THE TINY GMAIL WORD AND MY OLD BEAUTIFUL EMAIL PAGE CAME BACK. EMAIL HAS BEEN TERRIBLE. YOU HAVE TO EXPERIENCE IT TO KNOW. MESSAGES ON THE SIDE ARE " NOT RUNNING DUE TO A LONG RUNNING SCRIPT" ALSO, "SOME-

THING IS NOT RIGHT", ALSO "NOT RESPONDING". TAKING FOREVER TO GET THE LETTER PAGE TO WRITE YOU, OR TO CLOSE, OR TO DO ANYTHING. JUST FELT BROKEN, AND NOW HERE IT IS BACK AGAIN. :) :) ALSO LOST MY SOUND AGAIN LAST WEEK, COMES AND GOES FOR NO REASON. ANYWAY, I WAS READY TO HIRE A COMPUTER GUY. MEANWHILE ENJOYING IT. I DID COMPLAIN ABOUT IT TO THE FRONTIER GUY THIS NOON TIME, MAYBE HE DID SOMETHING WITH THE TECHNICIAN. GOING TO BED AROUND 6:30. ALWAYS LOOOOOVE, MOM

I saved 246 emails from Mom beginning in January 2019, a daily compendium of her life story. It was around this time that I began to save all her best photos to distribute at her funeral. I wish I had saved more voicemails. And I really hoped we could accomplish the project of recording her experiences over the course of 90 years, from the ice man's wooden cart to her accomplishments in learning how to use a computer. That was our plan for 2022.

What's that saying? *How do you make God laugh? Tell him about your plans.*

It's the good morning and good night of each day that bookends the beauty of and appreciation for living with gratitude and enjoyment. Recognition of a 'normal day' as the benchmark for hours well lived.

Perfection is overrated.

X. Funeral, Not Funeral

Gone

So this is what it feels like to be a motherless child,

losing the North Star, Sun and Moon,

Anchorless, Homeless, Heartsick.

Someone told me the depth of sorrow is equal to

the depth of love given and received in a lifetime.

And so, I must rise up to summon a most fortunate child

embraced by her goodness, kindness, compassion, strength,

the hugs she placed in my pocket knowing this day would come.

Love without judgment, giving without expectation of return,

understanding the beauty of humanity in all its forms,

finding joy in every single daily blessing, large or small.

She set the path for others to follow, in sickness and in health,

embracing life with a single command ... to care

for one another.

-*Susan MacNeil*

I'm not sure what caused Mom to change her mind so dramatically about her funeral planning. As a devout Catholic, I expected that she would want calling hours, followed the next day by a mass, the burial, and then a reception for everyone.

But the longer she lived, the less interest she had in pomp and circumstance. And she discovered that attending mass on television several times a week from the comfort and privacy of her recliner had even more personal meaning than the usual Sunday practice.

When she turned 89 she told me that she had changed her mind about a funeral. She no longer needed a mass or to take two days out of our lives to say goodbye. After visiting the funeral home to make arrangements, she decided that it was plenty nice enough to simply accommodate calling hours and remembrances followed by a cemetery burial. She wanted the sad event to be as easy as possible for us.

"Find a Catholic priest to say a few prayers graveside and that will be it," was her instruction.

And she didn't want a big reception that cost a lot of money, but a celebration of life at some later date. A party. So that was the plan.

The funeral home she chose was the perfect facility and even had a working fireplace, which was wonderful considering that the temperature on February 14, 2022 was 18 degrees with a wind chill factor of zero.

I planned the event as I had planned the dozens of events I'd organized over the course of my nonprofit career. But this one had to be perfect and reflect the life of our mother – a recognition of her legacy as light and love. Organizing all the details was both cathartic and devastating. It was a good distraction from the formality of wrapping up the nuts and bolts of her life in my role as executor.

But by the time the morning of February 13 greeted me, I was numb, almost too paralyzed to even pack. The night before I lay prone under the covers trying to tell myself that none of this was real. That Mom was still alive, and I hadn't been hauling out her house for days. That I hadn't actually spent the last 18 minutes of her life on the phone begging the heavens to miraculously restore her hearing since modern technology had failed her.

But at 6:00 am when the alarm went off, reality was undeniable. I felt nauseous and anxious, sure that I'd forgotten to prepare some important element, or that I'd trip and fall as I loaded bags into the car. I could hear my mother's voice in my head … "For God's sake, hang onto the railing and don't fall!"

While drinking my espresso I drew a ceramic star from the bowl on my kitchen table. I needed guidance, but what was revealed to me seemed completely counter-intuitive. The word shared with me was, Dance. What the heck was there to dance about? I felt cheated. Enjoying a merry moment was not in my plan for the immediate future.

By 8:30 am, the back seat of the car was brimming with my overnight bags, and I had not fallen. I started the car, sat in the parking lot, and actually felt like I had forgotten how to drive. Traffic was sparse, but I hesitated to get on the road because my brain seemed disconnected from my body. My hybrid car, normally very quiet anyway, soundlessly floated over the paved surface. By the time I reached the highway access five miles away, I was actually afraid to bring my car up to speed. I said aloud, "Mom, I don't know if I can do this. You have to help me."

I'd been making the drive with the radio blaring. Music from the 60s that came to me automatically, without thinking. But today I didn't want music. Today was all about crying, tears that just wouldn't stop. And remembering to breathe.

Accustomed to seeing a hawk or two during the drive, I was not surprised to see one almost immediately on my right. And then, on my left, another one. A third on my right. A fourth on my left, dead, its wings vertical as though saying hello. And then a fifth. By the time I'd driven 30 minutes to the Massachusetts border, I'd seen five hawks.

This was incredibly unusual. I'd never seen five hawks over the course of the entire drive. They were large sentries, white breasts demanding my attention from treetops and guiding me forward. Guardians meant to show me the way.

And I would have been happy with these signs alone. But by the time I reached Northampton, MA, I'd seen another ten. Four more by Springfield. Soon I crossed into Connecticut and by the time I veered off at exit 44, I'd seen another three. A total of 22 hawks made sure that I paid attention and traveled safely to my destination.

That number was, of course, the same number of eagles that Mom told me she had seen during an afternoon outdoor siesta. I'd questioned her information, substituting Canadian Geese for eagles. She was insulted. "I think I'm old enough to know the difference between eagles and geese," she replied.

But now she had the last laugh. And I obeyed her wishes to dance, seat-dancing in my car, laughing out loud.

"Show off," I said aloud. "You win."

As I rounded the exit ramp, something else caught my eye above the left of the windshield. It was white. Not just white, but pure, brilliant white. At first I thought it was a wayward seagull. But it wasn't large enough for a seagull. A prism of light emanated around it which I figured was reflection from the sun. Yet it resembled the iconic representation from every Catholic image of my youth. Without stopping to analyze my immediate reaction I said out loud, "No, that's a dove. And I'm plenty old enough to know the difference between a seagull and a dove."

Tears filled my view, and when I looked up again, it was gone. But the crystal clear image remains to this day.

It was definitely a dove.

I was sure that Mom had given me her final blessing, a gift to help me move toward the final chapter. Just like every other first throughout my life, she was by my side. I was reminded of the prayer she taught me to say each night before bedtime.

18 Minutes

"Oh, Angel of God, my guardian dear,

To whom God's love entrusts me here,

Ever this day be at my side,

To light and guard, to rule and guide.

Amen."

On the morning of February 14, the funeral home was ready for us to arrive early, so when we got there at 8:15 am everything was in place. Valentine's Day. The candy I brought had been placed in bowls. The staff was accommodating without hovering. Viewing the open casket was a revelation about how unnecessary and potentially disturbing it actually is to see the shell of your loved one devoid of spirit. Of heart and soul. Justin was so right.

I was glad we kept it open for only 30 minutes, and I stood by ceremoniously as the director lowered her body into the casket before it was closed. I said goodbye to this formation of skin and bone which bore no resemblance to the 68 years of love I had in my life. But it was oddly helpful to watch the process, like a child, needing to have the visual reminder of the final end. Once the casket closed, I could breathe again.

Is it weird to say that a remembrance event should be recalled as one of the best events of your life? I will not forget a single embrace, tear, shared story, loving admiration. My mother's legacy was one of kindness and generosity. Of unadulterated love. Visitors appreciated the takeaway photos (which the funeral director thought was an idea to share), the smiles she chose for people to remember, and the black and white display of her childhood and youth.

There she was in the Kiss Me Kate cast photo, my father in the chorus, hovering above her in the last row wearing a black beret. In another one she is holding a bouquet of roses while taking a bow. And as a child, standing next to the goat cart after having taken a ride. I wished I had photos of her scrambling up on the back of the ice man's wooden cart, scooping up ice shards on a hot summer day. Or holding a bag of warm peanuts while watching the organ grinder's monkey.

She was beautiful while posing along the Cabot Trail on her honeymoon. And where had she been for one completely candid shot of her smiling and laughing in a sleeveless blouse as she sat on the ground?

When it came time for remarks, my two brothers and I reflected about her in our own personal styles. We were good children who honored our mother with heart and soul. Guests also had their own special recollections. Friends drove from far distances to attend. Although I was initially dreading greeting everyone because I felt so depleted, that was not at all how it felt. I had been in isolation for four weeks in order to deal with Mom's illness, death, subsequent responsibilities and my shock and grief. My heart melted with each hug and helped fill the emptiness with love.

As the remarks began, my son reached over to grab my hand. It was completely unexpected. We did not look at one another, but held tightly, our enfolded fingers sitting on his knee. We stayed this way until I got up to share my comments. He sought that familiar connection again when I sat down.

And there was an unexpected realization about holding a funeral in the time of a pandemic. The mask requirement meant that with each embrace we had no choice but to look deeply into the eyes of the person sharing their love. No distraction, just intense connection. It was as though hearts melded in a way that wouldn't otherwise have happened. And it, too, was beautiful.

Shortly after Noon, the pallbearers were given instruction and carried the casket to the hearse. Mom did not want a limousine so I was first in line behind the hearse and others followed for the 30-minute ride to the cemetery in our hometown. In my rearview mirror, I saw that other passing vehicles on the road had turned their lights on to acknowledge the somber procession.

It had snowed lightly and because it was so cold, the white covering froze on the ground at the cemetery. A brutal wind created a frigid atmosphere in contrast to our warm hearts. But the cloudless sky was bright blue and the sun shone down.

The priest hailed from Hawaii, and in his thick accent, he made a joke about the winter cold before he launched into his perfunctory graveside service. It reminded me of every mass I'd attended as a kid, when we recited Hail Mary, Our Father and listened to the rat-a-tat recitation of the priest offering blessings. I'd heard that there is a serious shortage of priests in the United States, and so, as a result, most of them in the last two decades have come from outside the country. It struck me at this moment that my childhood priests, Father Bernard and Father Miller, somber old white men who commanded eyes up front, had been replaced by an entirely new generation of officiants.

In the course of his blessing, Mom received two rounds of holy water, which I know she must have appreciated. Twenty minutes later, it was over. Her name was already inscribed on the headstone next to my father's, but the date of her death would be done later that spring in time for her celebration of life.

And then it was time to go. Lingering in the freezing temperature was not an option. I drove by our old house, now disgracefully falling down, and remembered a childhood slideshow of wholesome, rural images instead. Of the lilac grove and summer breakfasts cooked on the grill out back. Why Mom delighted in placing a cookie sheet on the grill and cooking eggs, bacon and toast, I will never know. But the smell was intoxicating, and the picnic table made by my father was accommodating. It began the day with perfection. I can still see her standing there in the sunlight, smiling, engaged in the priority of being a mother and feeding her children.

After the internment, I returned to Mom's apartment to gather my belongings from the night before, and then headed to the funeral home for the photos, guest book, etc. When I arrived, the items had already been packed for me. I reached out my hand to offer my gratitude, and the funeral director invited a hug instead.

"Thank you for allowing us to provide comfort to your family during this difficult time," he said.

Be sure that you choose a funeral home with people who understand their job is to get you through a difficult day, one that then offers thanks for allowing them to comfort you.

It was late afternoon when I got on the highway for home. Only one hawk greeted me as I got onto the interstate. The full moon appeared in the distance, the glorious Snow Moon. The message from Mom was clear.

You're on your own now. I'll light the way. You'll be all right.

My Remembrance

I don't feel like I need to talk about Mom's capacity for love because everyone in this room was fortunate enough to know that she loved them. And today we feel the depth of that void, now that she is gone.

When the doctor first called me from the ER to say he didn't think she had more than 48 hours to live, he put her on the phone but she wasn't able to have much of a conversation. I was sobbing and she was having trouble breathing. So she gave me the high points in three phrases – remember I love you all, just go into neutral, and make sure everyone is okay.

So in an effort to make sure everyone is okay, I'd like to share some thoughts about Mom that will make you smile as you remember her time on this earth.

Occasionally she would lament the fact that in her old age she had developed 'addictions,' that was her word. Here are a few of them.

Coffee ice cream. The flavor reminded her of her youth in Massachusetts. She would devour a couple of gallons of coffee ice cream every week. And it had to be Friendly's ice cream. Nothing else would do.

Newspaper clippings. Even though she appreciated the power of googling any subject, or 'arrowing' as she called it, she could not resist printed articles. 9x12 clasp envelopes were everywhere in her house and on the front of them she wrote, "Important!" "Super important!" "Exercises To Do Now!" They were filled with recipes, advice for every conceivable problem, homeopathic remedies from gin soaked raisins to tart cherries and raw honey. Salt water gargling for a sore throat, tooth and gum problems. White vinegar for itching. During a recent hospital visit her leg itched and the nurse brought her some cream. But Mom couldn't resist. "If I was home I'd use white vinegar. It's amazing. Stops the itch. I have a gallon of it. Maybe you should think about using it."

Chocolate caramels. But only the softest caramel and only milk chocolate. Ghirardelli chocolate caramels were her favorite. She could polish off two bags in an afternoon while watching a Hallmark movie.

The weather. Our daily emails always included conversation and warnings about the weather, hers and mine, once she figured out how to Google both of our zip codes. "For God's sake, hang onto the railing and don't fall!" was her constant winter refrain.

Lobster rolls. She knew exactly where to find the best lobster roll for the price. Once home, she would split the lobster meat in half to enjoy two meals to get a 'bigger bang for my buck.'

She believed she was living in incredibly historic times and became a news junkie. Rachel Maddow was her nighttime trusted friend. The internet provided endless information. She was appalled at the 2016 election and relieved in 2020. She cried at the way immigrants were treated and applauded every news conference given by "that handsome President Biden." She would call me at work so I could hear the breaking news, turning up the volume and placing the phone next to the screen.

She loved to lay outside for an afternoon nap, talking with neighbors Judy, Nellie or Anna Mae while she watched the clouds and the birds. One day she told me she counted 22 eagles. "Eagles? Are you sure they were eagles? Not Canadian geese?"

Her chilly reply was, "I think I'm old enough to know the difference between eagles and geese." What could I say to that except, "I'm sure you do. And if anyone was going to see 22 eagles, it would be you."

We never got to take the final big trip she requested, which was "to see the ocean one last time." I'd planned a week's worth of traveling for us but when she fell last July, her injuries and concussion prevented us from going. Still, she was determined to make it this summer when she regained her strength. It took her five months of incredible perseverance to make enough progress for a day trip to celebrate her 90th birthday in November. And she believed until just before she died that the ocean was definitely in her cards this summer.

So I will make that trip myself in memory of her. I'll watch the waves and remember all our family vacations at the beach. I'll watch the clouds and know she is looking down on us with love. And I will definitely eat a lobster roll, saving half, as she did, for tomorrow.

-Susan MacNeil

You Must be a Saint if...

You figured out how to stretch a Pratt and Whitney blue collar salary to support a family of six.

You made sure all your creditors got paid something, even if it was only a few dollars a month.

You raised four children using cloth diapers in a house with only one bathroom and sketchy plumbing.

You made sure your children were clean and dressed for church every Sunday.

You budgeted for a donation to the church every week even though there wasn't really any money for that.

You raised four children basically all by yourself since your husband worked second shift and every other weekend.

You read to your children every day when they were young to make sure they got a good start in school.

18 Minutes

You brought us kids to the town beach in the summer even though you didn't drive. You were always bumming rides for us from your friends.

You told the owner of the store in South Coventry, that we went to after church, that it wasn't nice that he sold girlie mags.

You didn't have a clothes washer and did the family laundry once a week at the laundromat in Manchester. A week's worth of dirty clothes for 6 people washed and dried and folded every Sunday night. And then did ironing and hand washes through the week. And us kids were good at getting our clothes dirty.

You planned and cooked great meals for us throughout the week. You made sure we had a good breakfast every day and lunches for school and bag meals for us if we were going on a trip.

After we were a little older you worked at a crappy part time cashier job at ShopRite in Manchester to bring in a few extra dollars for the family.

Later you went into business for yourself cleaning houses. You got your driver's license and contributed to the family income substantially.

You talked to and helped total strangers all the time, whether it was picking up hitchhikers, or bringing people to your home, or complimenting families on their beautiful children, you did what most would not.

You supported us in everything we did and guided us through our formative years.

Love you, Bill

-Bill MacNeil

XI. Amplified Phones

"Reach out. Reach out and touch someone."

—Classic AT&T Advertising Jingle

The personal trespass of January 25, 2022 will never heal for me. I know that might sound like a dramatic pronouncement, but it's the truth. No amount of passing time will lessen the blow.

Reliving those last 18 minutes of Mom's life, able to hear the anguish in her voice while she could not hear mine, disturbs me like being a bystander at some horrible accident. You know what's coming but are unable to do anything to intervene.

Hanging onto the end of the phone without being able to fly through the line to Mom's side feels like desertion. Screaming so she could hear me was contrary to how we interacted with one another. Somehow I stand accused. Dereliction of duty. Bad daughter. And no matter how much I tell myself this is untrue, the sense memory is devastating.

I'm not so delusional as to think, for a moment, that I had control over the end of Mom's life. But the knowledge that her inability to hear me was so completely preventable haunts me, a devastating waking nightmare.

I'm someone who acts. And so I documented the experience of contacting the hospital's patient advocacy office in real time. For the record. The ignominy of that office calling me after Mom had already died to indicate they would be 'working on the issue' was further proof that these departments are often not carefully invested in the personal truths of complainants. I accepted the fact that this was the same old shit, different day, and returned to the depth of my pain.

And I was willing to let it go, considering the disappointing response. Until I received this letter dated on the day of her death.

Susan MacNeil, 95 Rockingham Rd. (should be Street, no period after the abbreviation for road), Bellows Falls VT. (no period after the abbreviation for Vermont)

Dear Ms. McNeil (misspelled last name),

Thank you for taking the time to let us know of your concerns regarding your experience at Hartford Hospital. We take these concerns very seriously and we are investigating the situation. Your patience is appreciated while we explore the details of the incident.

You will receive a letter in response regarding the review of this matter within 30 days of receipt.

I apologize that we failed to meet your expectations. We appreciate your feedback and the opportunity to address your concerns. Please do not hesitate to contact me if you would like to discuss this matter further or have any additional concerns at the Office of Customer and Patient Relations...

My proofreading observations were one thing. Somebody should ensure that whomever is handling correspondence to annoyed individuals while creating a form letter at least gets the basics right.

But beyond that, my reaction was explosive. How dare they treat my dire experience and personal distress as though I was complaining about the food? Had they not read and understood the content of my emails? I sat with this new observation until January 31, when once more I was compelled to act by going to the top of the food chain. If anyone needed to know about what occurred, it was the CEO.

31 January 2022

Jeffrey Flaks, President and CEO
Hartford Healthcare
1 State Street
Suite 19
Hartford CT 06103

Dear Mr. Flaks,

On Wednesday, January 19 my mother, Jean A. Brady, was taken by ambulance to Hartford Hospital. Her heart condition was thought to be dire upon her arrival, and I appreciated speaking with several doctors who realistically kept me informed of her situation.

Fortunately, the best possible bad news was provided the following day and she was admitted to the ICU. Medically fragile, she was monitored for all possibilities and cared for by an excellent team of doctors and nurses. When she pointed out that the usual bedside phone didn't allow for her to be able to hear conversations, she was brought an amplified phone that did the trick.

On Sunday, January 23, she was moved to C-10, the cardiac floor, because she had made some improvement. Although this floor did not allow for the same attention as the ICU, my 90-year-old mother understood and knew enough to ask for help while apologizing for bothering the staff in doing so. Medically, I felt she was still being monitored appropriately, and we both hoped she would be able to return home by the weekend.

The biggest issue we faced was the phone. Once again, she could not hear a thing, and it was becoming an impediment to keeping her calm, with her blood pressure low. I reached out to everyone who walked into her room on Sunday and again on Monday, to ask that an amplified phone to be brought to her side. Each person said they would follow up, and I hoped that if I made enough people aware, this would actually happen.

Around 11pm on Monday, 1/24, I followed up by calling the nurse's desk to ask again if the phone had been provided. It had not. I suggested that someone might simply bring it down from the ICU for her, and I was told that this would be investigated.

At 7 am on Tuesday, 1/25 I called again to ask the same question and was told that maintenance did not have one. Not a single amplified phone in all of Hartford Hospital. This did not sit right with me, and having been the Executive Director of an AIDS Service Organization in NH for 15 *years, I knew my next step was contacting Patient Advocacy. I crafted an email to this office, insisting that an amplified phone be found and delivered to Mom's room.*

At 7:20 am I received a call from my mother. She said, 'Honey, I'm so sorry to have to tell you this but I think I'm dying." For the next 18 minutes I stayed on the phone with her. We could not have a conversation because she couldn't hear me. I could only stand in her kitchen and continuously scream I Love You at the top of my lungs, repeatedly, so she knew I was there. As her pain escalated, nursing staff was absent due, apparently, to shift change needs. Finally after 15 minutes I called the front desk on the home phone and, hysterically, told them that Jean Brady in room 63 was dying and someone needed to get to her. At 7:38, my cell phone was disconnected. I crafted another email to Patient Advocacy to provide an update, but it was in vain. Somewhere around 8am, Mom was gone.

I have included copies of the emails I sent. These final 18 minutes are like a horror story that will never leave me. Just when I think I'm on top of my grief, I relive those moments when she couldn't hear the inflection of my voice or allow us to converse in a meaningful way.

I understand that your job has to be of epic proportions. I imagine that usually consumers write to you with complaints about medical practice. But that is not my intention. Mine is, in many ways, worse. It addresses a simple, obvious need that turned into a completely unnecessary nightmare because, for some unidentified reason, an amplified phone could not be found.

Mom was completely lucid, and because of that she had things to say. Important things at the end of her life. Like which Valentine's Day card I should send to which great-grandchild in the event that I inherited her beloved Birthday Book. She even informed her doctor that she knew her temp was the result of a bladder infection and told him what medication she should take. The first two tests returned negative, but Dr. Ahmed was so impressed with her intelligence and composure that he ran the test a third time. Sure enough, this time it was positive.

Today I received the most insulting template letter from Patient Advocacy, indicating you take concerns seriously and including an apology because you did not meet my expectations. If this was supposed to make me feel that anyone actually cared, you failed. This boilerplate language is meant to calm down the person who reflected an experience that was unsatisfactory in some way. Nothing more than a pat on the head and, "There, there, dear."

In addition, upon my return to my mother's apartment after I sat with her in the hospital, I received a call at 1 pm while standing in the same spot where I screamed at my mother for 18 minutes, the incongruous activity of screeching while expressing love. It was Maria from Patient Advocacy, telling me she received my email and was going to work on the problem.

"Don't bother," I replied. "Didn't you read all my emails? My mother is dead." I hung up the phone and forwarded the second email to their office.

This lack of careful attention to response, along with the letter I received today, tells me that despite all your efforts to make Hartford Healthcare an extraordinary place – and again, medically it is – you are missing the boat when it comes to the little, most important human things. Like genuine, personalized correspondence. And having enough damn phones to distribute to an increasingly aging hospitalized population.

The response indicates that I will hear from you in 30 days. The only satisfactory, acceptable response will be that you have found the money to purchase at least 1000 amplified phones and have distributed them to each floor of your entire hospital across all buildings, so that someone else doesn't have to live through what my mother and I lived through. Ever again.

I sent it off certified, so that receipt would be documented, wondering what response would follow from the guy in charge. On February 8, still planning for Mom's funeral on the 14th, my phone rang and the caller ID indicated Hartford Hospital. Could this be a call from his office?

It wasn't. The woman identified herself as the person who oversees patient relations, and she hoped to speak with me about the letter I sent to Mr Flaks. Given that I was on the verge of a breakdown at that point, I decided to simply show up in all my pain and vulnerability.

Fortunately, she behaved like a human being. She offered no excuses and repeated that I had identified an issue not currently on their radar, but that would now rise to the top of their list. I have to admit that she hung in there with me like a pro, part grief-counselor, part responsible administrator. When she told me that she would be addressing this matter immediately, I dared not hope for a response sooner than late Spring. I figured that likely this might be the only interaction coming my way and tried to channel my mother's philosophy in being grateful to hope that, at the least, something good might happen.

The following weeks were consumed with continuing to pack up Mom's apartment and planning and attending her services. I had placed on the back burner any thought of a follow-up to the phone call I received. Better to have no expectations and then be pleasantly surprised. So, to receive a follow-up letter from this woman dated February 23 felt almost miraculous.

Dear Ms. MacNeil,

First and foremost, I want to express again our deepest sympathies for the loss of your mother. Thank you for taking the time to speak with me about your experience with Hartford Hospital. I want you to know that your experience resonated deeply with me, and I worked with other leaders to ensure that what you have brought to our attention is rectified for future patients and families.

We deeply regret that we did not have the appropriate amplification device available when you were speaking with your mother. As a result of your experience, we recently ordered a supply of amplified phones that will be available to our patients. We are working to ensure that there is a process in place to replenish the stock as necessary. While we understand that this action cannot change your experience, I hope you will take comfort in knowing your advocacy on behalf of your mother will positively impact future patients and families. At Hartford HealthCare we act ethically and responsibly and hold ourselves accountable for our behavior and it is my hope our response to your concern has demonstrated that commitment.

Ms. MacNeil, we sincerely apologize for these disappointing moments in your experience with Hartford HealthCare. Your comments have given us an opportunity to look inward and continuously strive to exemplify our core values of caring, integrity, excellence and safety. If you have any further questions...

I could feel Mom beaming, happy that someone else would not have to suffer the same memory as that of our last 18 minutes together. And so if advocating for her unmet need resulted in goodness for others, I accepted the fact that this was the intended outcome all along.

My fervent wish is that every healthcare center understands that although medical attention is a critical necessity, it is just as important not to forget about the need for human connection — the one thing, particularly in times of stress, that makes life bearable.

What AT&T said. "Reach out and touch someone."

XII. Funeral Home

I can't stress this enough. Be sure to visit your chosen funeral home in advance to make important decisions ahead of time, and ensure that they will be able to provide what you need in order to survive the day.

This is the punch list for executor decision-making before, during, and after death. It's my personal observation meant to provide helpful hints about how to manage the difficulties of burying someone you love.

Casket – Choose the casket. Including a burial vault means that you can be buried at any time of year because a boom crane comes in to place it in the ground. But you have to make sure that the cemetery does year-round burials as well, which can impact the date of the service. And be sure to check with your funeral home's policy on accommodating a biting winter day to ensure that the chairs are wrapped in fleece covers, and they will provide a fleece blanket to ward off the wind and cold.

Casket Open or Closed – You decide if you want an open or closed casket. There can be private viewing hours for the family if you wish. But having seen Mom in an open casket, my vote is an emphatic no. The shell in the receptacle didn't even resemble my mother. Something to do with the mouth, which no longer has the ability to remain in an actual closed position. The sense of emptiness was overwhelming and underscored the truth of how it's our spirit that is shared with others, not our bodies.

Calling Hours and Service – You can do both on the same day or different days. You can opt out of a service and just do calling hours followed by remembrances and burial.

Death Certificates – The funeral home will provide four copies. Cost included. But if you need more, you can request them.

Social Security – The funeral home will notify SSA of the death. If SSA direct deposits for the following month, it will automatically be rescinded when they receive the death notice from the funeral home. If funds are used, they will have to be repaid to SSA. So pay attention to the deceased's checking account.

Payment – In Mom's case she provided copies of her life insurance to the funeral home. The easiest thing to do was to assign the proceeds to the funeral home, who will contact the carriers to notify them of her death so they can be paid. If money is left over, it is provided to the family.

Obituary – Obituaries are expensive! Each newspaper is different. I wanted to include the *Boston Globe* but it would have cost over $2000. As it was, for the *Hartford Courant and Journal Inquirer* the cost was $1100. You can create your own following a template, or ask the funeral home to help with standard language. Provide a photo. Color photos become cost prohibitive for the average person. Cost included.

Prayer Cards – The funeral home will design the card according to your wishes. They have a book with all the possible designs and prayers, or you can provide your own. Cost included.

Program – I opted to create a program to hand out to guests. Not everyone does this, but it's possible. The funeral home did a beautiful job printing it for me. Cost included.

Guest Book – The funeral home provides. Cost included.

Music – The funeral home will create the music background according to your wishes. Cost included.

Bottled Water – Funeral home provides. Cost included.

Tabling – Space will be provided for a photo arrangement, or a photo board, or a computerized scrolling display. You provide the finished product.

Easel Photo – The funeral home will enlarge the photo and place it on an easel next to the casket. Cost included.

Podium and Microphone – The funeral home will provide for remembrances. Cost included.

Priest – The funeral home will contact whomever you wish. Cost included.

Gravestone Engraving – The funeral home notifies the company who will then update the headstone, not necessarily in time for the service. Cost included.

Cemetery Burial – The funeral home takes care of all notification and advance planning. Cost included.

Date – The funeral home will negotiate the date with you. In our case, given upcoming storm activity, long distance travel planning needs, ongoing pandemic unknowns and older guests, and since a weekend wasn't open immediately, we chose Monday, February 14. Valentine's Day could not have been more perfect for Mom.

Embalming – The funeral home embalmed Mom for the open casket viewing. Cost included.

Timing – You can choose the timing with the funeral home – morning, afternoon, evening.

Casket Spray – Family orders and pays for. Funeral home will recommend a florist if necessary.

Meet with Director – As the executor, I felt so much better after meeting with the funeral director. I brought Mom's clothing to him, and he took an hour to review the decisions she had made and every detail of the contract. Seeing the space and her choice to use this particular facility was reassuring.

So that's the funeral home. Now here's everything else. Of course, seek your own professional legal advice if necessary.

Probate – Because Mom did not own any property, stocks, vehicle, etc. I was told there was no need to even contact probate. Otherwise, you would have to go through probate. This office is usually located in the town hall. It's a big process and can take months.

Wallet – When I went through Mom's wallet I found everything I needed and then some. Business cards for her chiropractor, hairdresser and doctors made it easy to contact them with the news that she was gone. She made me promise I would do this. And they appreciated it.

Banking – MAKE SURE that as an executor you are named on the primary banking account. It was very easy for me to go into the credit union, verify my signature and get a debit card in my name after her death to access the funds. But if there was a lot of money to consider, or investments and other items were being sold, you would have to set up a separate Estate account. Credit Unions don't do this, but banks do.

Financial – This is a big one. You must collect all credit cards and any current financial records reflecting bill payments. As statements come in, the balances either need to be paid, or you can advise that the estate doesn't have enough money to pay the balance. As a family member you are not responsible to pay the balance, unless you are a co-signer on the account.

Send each of the three credit reporting agencies a letter and include a copy of the death certificate so that they know the person is deceased. Apparently it is a sad truth that vultures scan the obituaries for the deaths of elders and then try to steal their identity. If this happens, and the credit bureaus have been notified, it will save headaches.

Apartment Cleaning Charges – We became aware of a very detailed list of cleaning expectations. For every task that is not completed to the satisfaction of the complex, there is a charge to the security deposit. I did not even think about this.

Rent – Mom insisted that I pay for another full month of rent in order to not be rushed and keep the utilities on. This was another unexpected gift. Having a place to sleep while going through all her belongings, and to accomplish the cleaning without the pressure of having a limited time to do everything was a godsend. It's inhumane to think this can be done in the span of a week or two during and after saying goodbye.

Mail Forwarding – Immediately forward all mail to the home of the executor so that final bills can be paid. This is easy to do online.

Computer – Mom used a computer for emails and Facebook. Know the password and username so you can check emails. But if the deceased and you both have a gmail account, and you no longer have access to the deceased's computer, then it becomes impossible to access the account from your home computer because the confirmatory text can't be sent to the deceased's email. And if you've already canceled the cell phone, then the same is true. I was surprised to learn this.

Vehicle – Bill had bought Mom a car, and originally it was in his name. But Mom signed over the title to him so that all he had to do was pick up the car and drive it back to Florida. She was so smart.

Neighbors – Mom lived in an over-55 complex so this meant she had lots of neighbors, each in their own apartment. She made sure I met and had the contact information for her closest friend there. That connection has been soothing and helpful. We were able to give her Mom's walker and electric recliner, which is what Mom had hoped. And she distributed the sad news to everyone.

If you have a parent who isn't as prepared as Mom was and doesn't insist that you attend When Mom Dies School, then do yourself a favor and initiate the conversation. Help organize all paperwork. Ask questions as they arise. Cry now and feel the pain to come. You will be glad you did when the fateful moment happens.

One last thing. Practice saying a few words out loud until you can do so without crying. Do this with profound respect, love and recognition of the reality. Death. Dying. Deceased. Funeral. Burial. Cemetery. Headstone. Cremation.

Because. Everyone. Dies.

EPILOGUE

I found so many notes and random writings in my mother's belongings. This must have been why she told me to go through each piece of paper in each envelope. Some of them I have placed earlier in this book. Some were written to her children while others were observations in the world. Some were dated, others not. Some are short stories. All are precious to me.

Our stories are important pieces of the puzzle we create each day. And when the final piece is laid in its exact spot, the one that has been waiting, what will the picture tell us? In the case of my mother, the remembrances of Mom shared at her service were exactly right. A devoted, loving mother whose life revolved around her children in the best possible way. A creative soul who soldiered on despite the challenges that arose. A woman whose heart always led her forward without regret. A deeply spiritual soul whose enduring faith promised that she had no reason to fear dying.

Some of the writings I found in her many clasp envelopes follow. They share her devotion to her family and the entire human race.

++++++++++++++++++++++++++++

Dear Susan, Bill, Don and Bruce – If I should die soon the greatest gift you can give me is to carry on and have the best life possible. You will always know how much you are loved and my spirit will always be near you. Forever love x a million, Mom

++++++++++++++++++++++++++++

I LOVE MY CHILDREN

I love my children,

I love them from the inside out.

They are in my sweat, my tears, my memories,

The purest love I have.

They are my past and my present, my fears and my laughter,

My breathing, my waking, my dreams, my looking back, my looking forward.

My God, my prayers, always my prayers, so much so you must be saying, Her Again?

Again!

My thousands of photos at 53, 55, 57, 59 – 224 years of memories and stories.

Of who we are, books keeping the love within, the seat of the soul.

I want everyone to be kind to them, to appreciate them, to know how wonderful they are!

To lovers, forgive as I watch and remember,

I don't mean to intrude as you look deeply into each other's eyes,

As you touch at this moment, when all the world is excluded.

If you smile at me or say hello, for just a second I am part of your specialness and I remember.

And to a parent, forgive me Mother of a child,

Thank you for not looking at me with disdain or suspicion if I talk to your child.

Or if I smile and your baby responds, for just a second I touch your world.

Thank you for being friendly, because I remember.

And to you at seventeen, will you ever know how beautiful you are?

Forgive me, I don't mean to intrude on your world,

A world of joy and pain, of secrets and longings, of fear and excitement.

When you don't turn away from me I am grateful for a smile acknowledging I exist.

Not in your world, but for a second I touch your newness and I remember my own,

And my children's

And all our hopes and fearlessness.

I remember.

(February 1997, Florida)

++++++++++++++++++++++++++++

March 2013

I'm surrounded by and with smiles,

They leap out at me from the frames,

My loved ones, my loved ones.

So blessed am I that I have them forever.

I have their beauty, their sweetness, their preciousness.

Charlie's mother has Susan's arms around her and they smile.

They are my angels – Debbie & Don, Kiyah, Bruce & Betsy & Aubrey,

Bill & Patty & Justin.

Charlie looks down and Justin hugs Kiyah and me.

And I have them with me, my grandchildren.

They all are near me and keep me company.

And the cards, signed with love, given with love, beautiful with love.

The albums, books of life times, years and years and years gone by.

Filled with proof of all it really was.

I can hold them in my hands, in my arms,

Their being is my life, my joy, my gift, everything.

How blessed am I, how thankful.

++++++++++++++++++++++++++++

2013

I am proud of myself and everything I've done.

I barreled through the hard hard days although I didn't realize that's what I was doing.

Only God could lead me to this sweet and special place,

And soon onto his amazing grace.

Kindness, caring, empathy.

Love is everything.

++++++++++++++++++++++++++++

2019

To 18 Watson Farm Drive,

You have sheltered me through the storms and witnessed the joy of adult children visiting ... of new babies joining the family. You have held me in your walls through illnesses so severe they seemed to say, no recovery, and yet I recovered. Through the heat of summers you kept me cool. Through the cold of winters you kept me warm.

You celebrated eight Christmases and eight Easters and multiple family birthdays. You saw me witness two weddings that made my heart sing with joy. You saw me share the love of neighbors and friendship. On sleepless nights your rooms comforted me. You watched as I made nutritious meals, blueberry cupcakes and cookies.

Eight years ago you welcomed me and as I start a new chapter, a part of my heart stays here. Saying hi and best wishes to your new occupant.
(Written when the plan was for her to move to Vermont, scuttled by the pandemic.)

++++++++++++++++++++++++++++

Dear Justin,

This is Jan 12, 1985. Your mother has given me a beautiful book to be filled out, giving information about ourselves, and the people who came before us. Like everyone else, there has been both a dark and light side to my life. I thought perhaps I would just talk about anything and everything. Just put it down, and someday it might interest you or someone. I won't even correct the typing mistakes, of which there will be many no doubt. The time span also will be any given moment, whatever comes to mind.

Right now I am thinking about any time during my childhood that seemed especially pleasant and memorable. Certain days, or hours stand out, as being extra enjoyable. When I was around three, I was read to and given books. They were about castles and 'little people' and so for years my imagination was filled with fairies, gnomes and princesses. In winter when the ice froze by the side of the road, I would imagine 'tiny houses' and villages for gnomes. The fields on both sides of my house, (new homes built in both fields) at 34 Westminster Ave in Watertown Mass became wonderful intricate places for fairies and gnomes to reside with flowers and stones and hills, all places for these little people to live.

My sister took elocution lessons and would learn her lines at home. Thru repetition, I picked up on some of it and this was deemed to show how 'smart' I was, and so I went to school at five years of age. I wish I had started school at six; the 'smartness' only lasted three years and then I started to have trouble in school. Not slow, but middle of the road – getting 70s instead of 90s. The school was St. Patrick's grade and high school, in Watertown Mass, taught by the nuns. At this time my brother was born, Robert Kenneth Guy MacKay. Five years younger than I. Marie, my only sister was five years older than I. My name was Adele Jean MacKay. My mother did not really like Adele so I was always called Jean.

Our school started at 8:30 am and went till 11:45. We walked home for lunch, at least a mile, and was back at school for the afternoon classes by 1pm. Over at 3pm. We would walk home. Some days we bought lunch, in the morning we had a break when we could buy juice or chocolate milk and stand at the front of the class and drink it. For some reason I was always a little afraid in school and this persisted the whole 12 years. My mother would make me sandwiches or canned chicken and to this day the smell of canned chicken brings back the memory of that odd fear.

When I came home on my noon break I would go into the field and pick a bouquet of wildflowers for my mother. That was a good feeling, it was a pretty field, and large to me then. Also the 'popcorn man' would walk up and down our street. He had a glass and metal cart that made popcorn and an old kettle filled with melted butter. For a nickel he would fill a bag with hot popcorn, a dash of salt and pour on melted butter. It was delicious!

We had a penny jar in the bedroom and could take what we needed. A penny candy store was on the left walking to school, not far from Waverly Ave. We'd stop for candy – then at the corner of Westminster, across the street was an ice cream store. We could buy a pint of ice cream and with a new funny book (now called comics) for a half hour we'd have pure relaxation on the front porch. Directly on the corner of Westminster Ave on the left going out, a distance of 3 stores, there was also a general store that sold ice cream. There it was a three-decker cone for a nickel a scoop. The cone was shaped like a shamrock, 3 scoops side by side.

We had a milkman with a horse drawn carriage. As the milkman came in, we'd go out to give the horse an apple or sugar or sweets. He seemed huge to me and so strong and powerful. Also a rag man went up and down the street calling out 'rags, rags for sale.' He would buy or sell rags for cleaning I guess. Then there was the ice man. We had an ice chest. My mother would put a card in the window with "pounds needed" indicated and however many pounds she wanted, the ice man would carry ice in on his back with ice tongs and over a rubber sheet on his shoulder.

When you think of it, a lot of business people were on the street. A man with a mule attached to a carriage with the date on it would go door to door. You could have your picture taken sitting in the carriage. My mother often took me to Boston on the trolley car. Boston was very safe then. The trip usually included a ride on the Swan Boats at the public gardens and if you went there today you would probably sit on the same swan boats I sat on, and we'd get a hot dog and large root beer in Grants 5&10. Sometimes we went to a movie. The theaters were so gorgeous you can't imagine how beautiful they were. As close to a real castle as you could get. All gold and velvet and crystal.

My father was Francis Edward MacKay. His father came from Scotland at an early age, I understand. He had a brother Bill who was shell-shocked in the war. (Read up on World War I) Bill died never knowing the war ended. My father had a brother Bob who we loved so very, very much. My father was blonde with blue eyes and smoked Camels. Bob was dark-haired with brown eyes and smoked a pipe that smelled delicious. He often held me on his lap. He and my father had a gentle, kind, loving nature, patient and quiet. They had a hard life and yet this was their nature…

I wish she had finished her thoughts for both Justin and me because these gems of a time gone by, her memories of daily living, are priceless and will never come again.

Encourage your loved ones to share their stories for posterity. Those are the only stories worth telling.

Obituary

Jean Adele MacKay MacNeil Brady, formerly of Coventry, Ellington and South Windsor, left this earth to fly with the angels on January 25, 2022 after sharing 90 years of kindness, compassion and love with everyone she met. She was born on November 11, 1931. In 1952, Jean married her high school sweetheart, Charles MacNeil at St. Patrick's church in Watertown MA. They met while performing in 'Kiss Me Kate' at Watertown High School. Her clear soprano voice won radio singing competitions in Boston and she enjoyed music all her life.

Together they raised four children over 35 years. Her devout Catholic faith never failed her. She enjoyed every beautiful moment and outing to the fullest. She was a greeting card fanatic and never missed an important occasion by making sure to send heartfelt wishes. Most of all, Jean gave without a thought of anything in return, whether it was her love, her time or her earthly goods. Giving away baked goods, especially blueberry cupcakes and brownies, made her smile (and her doctors always appreciated the effort). She harbored no grudges, sought the best in everyone, and her smile made you believe in goodness, light and love. Jean personified joy, beauty and determination.

Jean and Charlie began their family in Massachusetts, moving later to Coventry CT, residing there for 31 years. After the death of Charles, Jean married James Brady and moved to Ellington CT where she resided for another 25 years and was a member of St. Luke's Catholic Church as a devoted parishioner and beloved Sunday School teacher. She relocated to Watson Farms in South

Windsor in 2012 and considered her neighbors a second family, especially Judy Stone. Computer proficiency allowed her to send daily emails and enjoy all her Facebook friends while never hesitating to pick up the phone for a personal conversation.

Jean is survived by her four children, Susan MacNeil of Bellows Falls VT; Bill and Patty MacNeil of Fort Myers FL; Don and Deb MacNeil of North Windham CT; and Bruce and Betsy MacNeil of Jamestown RI. She adored her grandchildren; Justin Ellsworth of Manchester NH; Michael MacNeil and his fiancé, Kadian Crawford of Miami FL; Jami MacNeil of Richmond ME; Kristine Reed and husband, Andy of Westford MA; Aubrey Brown and husband, Arin of Tallahassee FL; and great-grandchildren Kiyah Glenn Ellsworth of Barcelona, Spain; Lydia, Hattie and Ada Reed; and Aurelia Brown and her new sister, Adelyn, who will arrive in February. Jean remained in close contact with her many nieces, nephews and their families.

She was predeceased by husbands Charles MacNeil and James Brady; brother, Robert MacKay; sister, Marie Walton; and parents, Evangeline and Francis MacKay. Public calling hours and remembrances will be held on Monday, February 14, 2022 from 10:00 am – Noon at the Carmon Funeral Home, 419 Buckland Road, South Windsor. Burial will immediately follow at St. Mary's Cemetery, Main Street in South Coventry. A Celebration of Life will be held in the Spring.

Jean was grateful for her life and those she loved. She will be so missed and yet, her indomitable spirit lives on in every soul she touched. In lieu of flowers, memorial donations be made to the South Windsor Senior Center, 150 Nevers Road, South Windsor

CT 06074. To leave an online condolence, please visit www.carmonfuneralhome.com.

Photo Album

Jean, with goat, age four

Jean, age five

Jean, curtain call, "Kiss Me Kate"

Jean's graduation photo

Jean on her honeymoon

The author, age four

Makeup bag artwork

Note from makeup bag

Jean, 2021

About the Author

Susan MacNeil grew up in rural Coventry, Connecticut with her three brothers, a wooded environment that invoked a sense of freedom to dream.

Nightly bedtime stories read by her mother birthed a love of words that dwelled restlessly in her pocket.

Vases filled with lilacs scented the living room while her mother sang love songs at the kitchen stove preparing breakfast before school.

There was never a doubt that family was at the center of her mother's universe.

Susan learned about goodness and devotion from her mother, and ultimately brought those qualities into her professional and volunteer activities.

18 Minutes is a labor of love to honor her mother, whose life was a constant example of generosity, kindness, beauty and understanding.

In the end, this is all that matters.

CPSIA information can be obtained
at www.ICGtesting.com
Printed in the USA
LVHW081343221222
735718LV00014B/581